PRAISE FOR
WHAT'S HE REALLY THINKING?

"Paula winsomely weaves together helpful insights and information in a very relatable book [written] for every woman who wants to grow in understanding and loving the men in her life."

—STASI ELDREDGE
Best-selling Coauthor, *Captivating*

"As a psychiatrist over the past thirty-four years, I have listened intently to the innermost secret thoughts and emotions of several thousand men and women, and I have a fairly good idea of how they think. But as I read Paula's book, I was amused, amazed, comforted, encouraged, convicted, enlightened, and even entertained by all the wonderful new insights she has blessed us with. The book not only describes men in general but specific types of men common in our society today, as well as how a woman can relate to them. I recommend that men also read this book so as to better understand themselves and their need to know how to better relate to the women in their lives.

I especially love the final question Paula poses to women at the very end of the book, 'At the end of your life, what would you want to be remembered for by the man you love? How would you want to remember him?' I would hope male readers would benefit their wives by asking themselves the same two questions."

—PAUL MEIER, M.D.
Founder, national chain of Meier Clinics
Author, *Love is a Choice* and *Finding Purpose Beyond Our Pain*

"Once you savor the words of this book you will find, like I have, a deeper appreciation of your man seeping into your soul. This just may be the best book written on understanding men."

—SUSAN ALEXANDER YATES
Bestselling Author, *And Then I Had Kids*, *And Then I Had Teenagers,* and *Barbara and Susan's Guide to the Empty Nest* (coauthored with Barbara Rainey)

"Only a woman with twenty years of counseling experience, who's been married to the same man for a long time, could give us the incredible insight into men that we get in Paula Rinehart's new book. Goodness knows the rest of us have tried! Thank you, Paula, for a wonderfully insightful, biblically-based guidebook into just how men think and why they do what they do. We may make light of our differences, but all women know this is a serious topic that, fortunately for us, gets addressed in a very real, very helpful way in this book. Make sure you take notes . . . and enjoy!"

—KIMBERLEY KENNEDY
Author, *Left at the Altar*

"I love this author. Fact is, I've read all her other books. Pithy, practical, realistic, God-honoring—I love her style. And I love this new book aimed at helping women understand the men in their lives. Being of the male persuasion, I'd have to say that her depth of insight into the male modus operandi is spot on. Reading it made me feel understood, accepted . . . down right enjoyed. Is it okay that I tell you that I wept a few times? I did. It touched me that deeply. And I'm just a reader, for goodness sakes. I can only imagine how the man in your life will respond to you when you begin to paint into your relationship the wisdom found in these pages."

—DAVE FRAHM, ND
Author, *Healthy Habits*
Health*Quarters* Ministries

READER RESPONSES

"To be intimately known and deeply loved . . . isn't that what we all long for? God has gifted Paula with the unique ability to glimpse into the souls of the people she meets. Her new book *What's He Really Thinking?* gives a fresh perspective and tender hope in a world of misunderstood relationships. With amazing and honest insight, Paula's words made me feel as if she had gently read my mind and heart and discovered truths, expectations, losses, and longings—some of which I was not even aware. Thank you, Paula, for encouraging me once again to trust and relax in the arms of the One who intimately knows me and deeply loves me!"

—MOLLY
Tyler, Texas

"This book opened my eyes to how I can hurt the man I love through my distance. I've made a new commitment to not roll up the welcome mat in my heart when I don't get the response I want from him. As I turn to Jesus who knows me and listens to me perfectly I can take the pressure off. I'm starting to realize that "need" is not a four-letter-word; it's some of the best respect I can give my husband."

—REBECCA
Irving, California

"When I first read the title of this book, my immediate question was, how on earth could a woman know what a man is thinking? We men don't tell *anyone* what we're thinking. But somehow Paula has figured out what's going on behind the closed doors of me and all my fellow y-chromosome holders. And even better, her book sets out to explain us, and to appreciate us, not to change us. Thank you, Paula, for 'spilling the beans' on why we do what we do."

—KEVIN
Wake Forest, North Carolina

"We so often hear those 'good-natured' jabs at men, belittling them for having a one-track mind or being so hard to understand. It's easy to just throw up our hands, roll our eyes toward the sky, huff "men!" and just dismiss those delicate differences. Paula is a rare voice that tells us to hold off on our judgment and actually *enjoy* the men in our lives *because* they are different. Her book is encouraging, thoughtful, well-researched, and full of the wisdom that comes from experience. As a single girl, I now see a different, kinder way of approaching the world of manliness . . . and I have some wisdom in my back pocket to pull out when I need it!"

—JENN
Knoxville, TN

What's He
REALLY
Thinking?

OTHER BOOKS BY PAULA RINEHART

Better Than My Dreams

Strong Women, Soft Hearts

Sex and the Soul of a Woman

Choices

Starting Strong

What's He
REALLY
Thinking?

*How to be a
Relational Genius
with the
Man in Your Life*

Paula
RINEHART

THOMAS NELSON
Since 1798

NASHVILLE   DALLAS   MEXICO CITY   RIO DE JANEIRO   BEIJING

What's He Really Thinking?

Published in Nashville, Tennessee, by Thomas Nelson. Thomas Nelson is a registered trademark of Thomas Nelson, Inc.

Thomas Nelson, Inc. titles may be purchased in bulk for educational, business, fund-raising, or sales promotional use. For information, please e-mail SpecialMarkets@ThomasNelson.com.

Unless otherwise noted, Scripture quotations are taken from NEW AMERICAN STANDARD BIBLE®, © The Lockman Foundation 1960, 1962, 1963, 1968, 1971, 1972, 1973, 1975, 1977, 1995. Used by permission.

Scriptures noted ESV are taken from THE ENGLISH STANDARD VERSION. © 2001 by Crossway Bibles, a division of Good News Publishers.

Scriptures noted MSG are taken from *The Message* by Eugene H. Peterson. © 1993, 1994, 1995, 1996, 2000. Used by permission of NavPress Publishing Group. All rights reserved.

Scriptures noted NIV are taken from HOLY BIBLE: NEW INTERNATIONAL VERSION®. © 1973, 1978, 1984 by International Bible Society. Used by permission of Zondervan Publishing House. All rights reserved.

Some identifying names and details have been changed to protect the identities of those involved.

Published in association with Wordserve Literary Group, Ltd., 10152 Knoll Circle, Highlands Ranch, Colorado 80130

Library of Congress Cataloging-in-Publication Data

Rinehart, Paula.
    What's he really thinking? : how to be a relational genius with the man in
your life / Paula Rinehart.
        p. cm.
    Includes bibliographical references.
    ISBN 978-0-8499-1880-3 (pbk.)
    1. Man-woman relationships—Religious aspects—Christianity. 2. Men—
Psychology. I. Title.
    BT705.8.R56 2009
248.8'43—dc22

                                                            2009001826

Printed in the United States of America

09 10 11 12 13 RRD 9 8 7 6 5 4 3 2 1

We are all of us calling and calling across the incalculable gulfs that separate us . . .

—DAVID GRAYSON

CONTENTS

ACKNOWLEDGMENTS

I am tempted to acknowledge every man I ever knew well, including old boyfriends, but I will spare the reader that recital.

My own two indefatigable tutors in the world of maleness have been the most obvious (and the most valuable): a small-town banker father who took me into his confidence early and, through a haze of tobacco smoke, eloquently narrated his experience of life. To this day, the smell of cigarettes cheers my soul like the best perfume, and I will always miss his humor and insight. My father self-destructed over the last ten years of his life. That tragedy left me with questions of which this book bears some of the fruit.

I am also grateful for a husband who has endured the persistent probings of a writer-wife seeking to get the why behind the what of the way men think. He is one long-suffering man.

Scattered in between is a good brother, a fantastic son, a talented son-in-law, and now a grandson who is not yet old enough to grow a mask and is therefore an uninhibited exposé. I hope to live long and die old so I can see the man Andrew becomes. These men have made me want to listen—and more important, in some limited way, to understand. They make me sit up straight on the inside and take good notes.

A natural curiosity has also left me indebted to a posse of male writers. To Robert Bly for the way he illumined a man's heart without turning sappy. To Gordon Dalbey for articulating the way God heals a man's soul. To George Gilder for his brilliant grasp of the psychological meaning of male sexuality. To Frank Pittman for letting us all in on his lifelong pursuit to describe the way men do life. To Andrew Comiskey for the piercing insights a man gains as he makes his way out of homosexuality. To Philip Yancey for sharing the impact of losing a father early. To Brent Curtis for his conviction that a man will never become who he actually is apart from the God who made him. And to John Eldredge for the way his writings and his person have fleshed out the substance and content of that truth. These men opened doors to a world in which I am a willing visitor until the buzzer dings and I return to my accustomed habitation, a woman's state of being. It's a familiar, spacious existence that's far better decorated, so to speak.

Last, and significantly, I am grateful beyond words to the host of men—good friends and counseling clients—who've entrusted me with their stories through the years. To those men especially, my gratitude for allowing us all to follow your path. You are the ultimate guides in "understanding men."

Chapter 1

UNDERSTANDING YOUR INFLUENCE

You make me want to be a better man.
—JACK NICHOLSON TO HELEN HUNT,
IN THE MOVIE *AS GOOD AS IT GETS*

If there is one universal in any woman's life, it's this: she will always be relating to a man.

Fathers. Friends. Husbands. Boyfriends. Employees. Sons. Men make up approximately half the human race—and many of them are up close and personal. This man in your life. Or this man you want to be in your life.

Since men are everywhere, it's easy to confuse the commonplace with the known and understood. But men are another species, really. Men care about different things. They are motivated by different drives. Their hormones shape their brains in ways alien to our own. Men aren't women with big feet and beards. They are completely *other*.

All of this to say—men are fascinating creatures.

I admit that there are days when men seem more frustrating

> *Men aren't women with big feet and beards.*
> *They are completely other.*

than fascinating. I've spent a big chunk of my life waiting for a man to respond as a woman would. But frustration is designed to give way to intrigue. Intrigue can serve us well. It leads to the questions that, I believe, are central to enjoying life with men: *Who is this man? And how does he experience life differently than I do?*

Your discoveries in this search can provide what you need in order to relate well to men. Most important, those clues will be the basis of becoming a relational genius with the men who matter most to you—especially the man you love.

My own search for understanding has been helped by my work as a professional counselor. I listen for a living, so I've heard many men tell stories about themselves that they don't tell easily. Thirty-plus years of marriage to a quiet, thoughtful guy of German descent means I've had to learn to read a man who (like most men) is a bit of an enigma.

Letting yourself puzzle over the mystery of gender, of men and women created as they are, for a purpose, has its rewards. It leads to a God so awesome that it takes two distinct genders—male and female—to even begin to express what he's like.

This larger picture is what you feel and intuit in many subtle forms. Think of the last time you sat with a steaming cup of coffee in a relaxed setting, talking with a group of friends. Women friends. (Chances are, much of that conversation was actually about the men in your lives).[1]

Have you ever noticed how the conversation changes the moment when, by some chance, a guy joins the group?

It's not the same, is it? Something *other* has arrived on the scene. It's more than the way he looks. It's not merely that the topic of conversation may suddenly shift. This man brings a presence that just feels . . . well, different. Let me suggest that exploring what and why it's different can unlock some of the richest secrets in relationships.[2]

One can argue that men are simpler beings, and that

> *We are better able to love what we understand. And loving and being loved is the main way we reflect the glory of God.*

may well be true. But the doors into their inner lives—their psyches—are not the same as yours and mine.

Understanding where a man is coming from takes some real detective work. The way I figure it, though, is this: we are better able to love what we understand. And loving and being loved is the main way we reflect the glory of God.

BY A STRANGE ROUTE

Understanding the man you love and loving the man you understand is greatly helped, oddly enough, by a sane estimation of yourself. As a woman, what you bring to a man is the antidote, the completion, the sheer pizzazz that, humanly speaking, he searches for all his life. Percy Sledge got it right a long time ago: when a man loves a woman, he'd trade the world for the good thing he's found.[3]

I bet there are days when you don't feel quite that special. And yet, a man with any insight knows he's missing something. We are usually the ones in the dark.

> *A woman,*
> *by her very nature,*
> *ushers a man into*
> *a world that, to him,*
> *is marked by beauty.*

It's crucial to realize the good and creative power God gives us women. As one guy on the verge of marriage said to the woman he loved, "You bring beauty to my life." His fiancée was surprised to hear his comment; she's not a woman known for her looks. He was right, though. A woman, by her very nature, ushers a man into a world that, to him, is marked by beauty.

Any reality check about your actual worth as a woman will take you back to creation. We are not the afterthought of God's original work, as if he stapled a few enhancements onto the original model for added value. John and Stasi Eldredge say well in their book *Captivating,* "[Eve] is the crescendo, the final astonishing work of God. Woman. In one last flourish, creation comes to a finish not with Adam, but with Eve. She is the Master's finishing touch. . . . Eve is created because things were not right without her. Something was not good."[4]

Indeed, some of the most famous words in the creation

account are the ones God speaks to Adam: "It is not good for the man to be alone."[5] That reality echoes through the chambers of time until it shows up in hard, cold statistics. Men who live alone, sans the company of a woman, die earlier and have greater rates of depression and suicide.[6]

Maybe that's why the Eagles sang about the "desperado" who needed to come to his senses and come down from his fences—he needed to let someone love him before it was too late. Otherwise, his prison would be "walking through this world alone."[7] And men just don't do well alone.

Without the influence of a woman—without mothers and

> *When a woman realizes her worth, she relates differently to a man.*

sisters and wives and daughters—a man lives like a "naked nomad,"[8] a rootless, purposeless existence, wandering the earth in search of himself. God said it wasn't good for a man to be alone, and so . . . he created a woman. Most men know in their gut that a woman's presence completes something inside that remains loose, unfocused, and disconnected without her.

Without you.

REALIZING YOUR WORTH

When a woman realizes her worth, she relates differently to a man. In fact, without that kind of confidence, it's hard to get accurate insight and understanding about men.

Listen to the story of a friend of mine, and consider how a sane estimate of herself shapes the way she relates to men. Her chutzpah is inspiring.

Hillary was beginning to date again after a failed first marriage, and this time she was clear about what she wanted in a man. She had been seeing a guy named Greg; she believed their relationship had real possibilities. Hillary was also a fabulous cook. Occasionally, she would bring her recipe book over to his place and cook something special for the two of them.

One night Hillary was at Greg's place, poring over her recipe, making sure she had all the ingredients. And Greg chose this moment to check in with her. "I've been thinking about you and me," he said, rather casually. "I'm happy with the two of us just being friends."

I should mention that, up to this point, Greg had given Hillary every possible signal that he was interested in a future with her. Certainly not just as friends. She had months of energy invested in this relationship. She had been clear, from the start, that she hoped to get married again.

So what did Hillary do? No tears, no big scene, no explosive drama. Hillary looked at Greg for a moment and paused, weighing the implications of what she just heard. Then she closed her recipe book, gathered up her stuff, and calmly walked past Greg, whose mouth was now ajar. She spoke only one sentence on her way out the door:

"Honey, you're going to miss me when I'm gone."

Now, there's a woman who has realized that what she

brings a man is something too valuable to be used up and discarded. It's too good to squander. She could win an award for "best one-liner delivered at a crucial moment."

There's a kind of push-back quality in good relationships between men and women. When a woman assigns the same value to herself that God does, she is able to ask something from a man: *Give me the best of who you are.* When we count our own influence, we're in a position to acknowledge a man's as well. We're a few steps down the road of understanding men.

EYES TO SEE

By far, though, your most profound influence in a man's life is an insight so familiar that you, perhaps, take it for granted.

A woman's brain can add together a raised eyebrow, the tone of someone's voice, the way his eyes avoided hers when a certain topic was discussed—and the impression she forms is, quite often, uncannily accurate. This ability has been honed from birth. Your mind comes equipped with antennae that gather a deluge of information, sorting and filing beneath your conscious awareness. More than you may think, you are lining up the dots that make it possible to know someone's interior world.

This ability can be intimidating to a guy. It's like you have on night goggles, and he's just stumbling along in the dark. But it's also rather wonderful. Your ability to see is an enormous gift to him. You may "get him" long before he gets you.

> *God has given you eyes to see. And those eyes can be a man's most reliable mirror of who he is and who he can be.*

Much of what he realizes about himself comes only as he works at a relationship with you. God has given you eyes to see. And those eyes can be a man's most reliable mirror of who he is and who he can be.

A bit of insight is what lets you see past a backward baseball cap—or the defeated expression of a guy with a remote in his hand. You recognize not just the persona but the potential. And sometimes, it's what you see that gives a man the courage to claim it for himself.

A variety of studies indicate that men are more easily satisfied in a relationship than women. I used to doubt that research. But after listening to men discuss their relationships, I realize the old adage is true: if a man gets a (reasonable) dose of good food and good sex, and if he can talk with the woman in his life rationally and without rancor—he's a pretty happy camper.

What most men learn of the *depth* that's possible between two people comes from an understanding and persistent woman.

So it's worth the time to explore this strange and wonderful world men inhabit. A man will let you into his domain if he's convinced you won't use his heart for a punching bag.

He longs for you to find his strength—and to need his

strength. In the deepest symbolic meaning of sexual intimacy, his great hope is that he will be received by you.

WHO IS THIS MAN?

If you've ever shopped for a man's or a boy's clothes, you know how fundamentally boring that task can be. *Give me a pair of jeans and a pair of khakis with two shirts, and I'm out of here.* Women's clothes are another story. The options are exhausting.

If we could peel back the layers of our inner worlds, though, we'd find that the stripes and colors and textures of a man's soul are quite richly varied. On the inside, they aren't all wearing blue jeans. Or khaki pants and a polo shirt. The actual shape of their interior lives varies greatly.

Our drives and passions make us who we are. Some of those we are simply born with—like wiring that is already installed, waiting on the hand of God to turn on the switch. As I mentioned before, the most telling question we can ask is, who is this man? If he were on a desert island with a handful of survivors, what kind of man would he be, because this is who he is?

There are many broad brushstrokes we could use to describe men. The ones I offer here are generalities, and if taken as such, they can prove useful.[9] The man you have in mind may be a combination of two descriptions. These are helpful categories because they describe the emotional and psychological "neighborhood" where this man lives.

THE FIGHTER

This guy is born itching for a cause. His best self is motivated by heroic impulses. A crusader at heart, he wants to be on the winning side of ideals he believes in. He's the state trooper you pray will find your idling car during a snowstorm. Terms like *loyalty*, *responsibility*, *willing to serve* describe the better parts of his character. He has more drive and energy than the average guy. His idea of "relaxing" might be stiff competition in a sport that leaves him a happy, sweaty mess. Take heart, though. In a relationship, he also won't let a woman he loves go without a fight.

Yet a "fighter" man gone awry closely resembles a pit bull. Anger can become a drug he uses to distance himself from any emotion that feels like weakness. God's work in his life will often cause him to find his strength not in himself but in God.

THE PROTECTOR

This guy appears to be more laid-back than he is. Some might fault him for a lack of initiative in a public sphere of influence. But his focus is those people and those responsibilities he feels particularly charged to protect. In that arena, he's part Labrador retriever and part bulldog, and he will defend his territory tenaciously. In a relationship, he can be moved by the pain you feel—especially if he thinks it's pain he caused or failed to prevent. When everyone else in your life has packed up and gone home, this man will still be there.

Left to his fears, the protector can tend to overcontrol the people he most cares about. He may collapse under a weight of responsibility he is afraid to delegate to others. Redemption, for him, looks like learning to let go and trust that it's not all on his shoulders. He may struggle to let others in very close.

THE ADVENTURER

When you think of an adventurer, think of Chuck Yeager breaking the sound barrier or the men who spent years trolling for the remains of the *Titanic*. The adventurer is a man driven by the need to explore the universe. He wants to be "out there in it." He's motivated to push out the bounds—to do it because it can be done. *Risk* is just another word for *challenge*, and he loves that. In a relationship, you (hopefully) become part of the adventure. He longs for a woman willing to join him as he explores some new physical terrain.

The adventurer can be naive about his own personal limits—or the limits of others. If he uses adventure to avoid the unpleasant aspects of relationships, he can mutate into a true escapist and the people he loves will feel abandoned. As with many things, his real challenge is balance and perspective.

THE BUILDER

Every human endeavor needs the builder. This man will invest his energy putting together the bricks and mortar, the people, or the conceptual systems needed to make something go. A big-picture thinker, he usually has a natural ability to get others to work together for a common purpose. You will enjoy life with a builder, as long as he creates a category called "building relationships," since those, too, are built piece by piece.

Life with a builder goes south if he gets fixated on his goal. His do-or-die attitude can alienate the people who matter most to him. It may be hard for him to wait on God, to believe that "unless the LORD builds the house" (whatever that may be), the labor will be for nothing.[10]

THE NURTURER

The nurturer is the consummate father figure. Put him in any setting, and he naturally becomes a sort of coach or mentor or spiritual shepherd. Others value him for his rocklike quality. He cares what happens to people; he feels charged with the responsibility of developing people within his influence. Internally, he has an uncanny sense of what's needed to help someone become who he or she is capable of being. What you may feel most concretely in his presence is the permission to exhale. It would really bother this kind of man if he feels he has failed or disappointed you.

A nurturing man gets off track when he confuses care with fixing or solving the problems of someone important to him. "You should . . ." or "You ought to . . ." might be words he uses too often. If his concern turns heavy-handed, he will spoil the freedom of those he loves.

THE REFLECTIVE

When you think of the reflective man, think of a guy driven by the quest for meaning. He might be part philosopher or part artist, but his internal push is to understand the big picture of life, and then to express what he sees in some form. Those close to him can make the mistake of thinking he is lazy. That is rarely true. He would love for you to be able to appreciate the challenge of his quest. His longing is for someone who can follow him through the labyrinth of his ideas and passions.

A reflective man, unredeemed, will be prone to despair. He may live isolated, at least internally, because he believes no one understands him. Finding God in his quest is particularly grounding for this sort of man. Focus and hope are his challenges.

THE SCIENTIST

This guy gets his happiness from some kind of brainy adventure. You might even call him an "intellectual adventurist." He will persist in a project until he finds an answer. He'll collect the data and organize the results for the payoff of inventing something or reaching a concrete conclusion. Only a few people may get what fascinates him. It's particularly important to him that you do—even if he seems too cool to care.

The scientist can feel defeated by the parts of life that stubbornly remain a mystery—or by the subtleties of relationships. He may struggle to let others out of a box he's created that's too tight.

As you read through these descriptions, you probably noted that there is an upside and a downside to each. God made each of us with his good purposes in mind. There is a redemptive expression of our personalities—God's glory as it shines through our particular cracked pot. So the question in the back of your mind as you relate to a man is always, how is this guy meant to bless and bring life?

> *The question in the back of your mind as you relate to a man is always, how is this guy meant to bless and bring life?*

But there is a downside. Though God creates for his purposes, and while those purposes are good, there are cracks in the pot. Broken places that bring pain. In a fallen world, there is always a downside. When trauma and fear and sin invade our lives, the best of who we are gets muted and twisted.

So every relationship—especially one between a man and a woman—is carved out in this gap between who we are meant to be and who we are in this moment.

The descriptions above are only the bare beginnings of understanding the man or the men in your life. I'm not suggesting it's your job to figure him out. It's more like an opportunity—a great, intriguing opportunity that pays great dividends to you both.

As you read this book, remember that while only 2 percent of your genetic structure is different from a man's, that 2 percent is still greater than the difference between humans and chimpanzees.[11] So it's not your imagination that men go at life in ways that are unlike yours.

There are so many fascinating parts to the puzzle that

makes up maleness. Really, each model should come with a manual. Then, maybe, it would not take so long to trace the edges of someone who appears so similar in his humanness—yet who is so different in his particularities.

We come to love what we understand. Follow me, then, into the intriguing world of men. Let them tell you their stories. Discover the distinctly male ways in which they feel pain or experience change. You will stumble on a new respect for the challenges men face. It's possible that you'll find yourself expecting more from a guy, rather than less. Finding a path through conflict will, hopefully, be a bit easier.

You may not consider yourself a total relational genius when you are done reading. But I promise you, the man you love will know something's up. And you will know your way around his world a whole lot better than when you began.

I think there's a decent chance he will return the favor.

PART ONE

<hr>

*Understanding the
Man You Love*

<hr>

Chapter 2

WHAT MEN DO

> *Then the LORD God took the man and put him into*
> *the garden of Eden to cultivate it and keep it.*
>
> —GENESIS 2:15

In the art of understanding men, there's something to be learned from younger guys. From boys, to be exact. Boys are a bit like miniature men with no camouflage in place.

Given that, let me share an experience I had with a six-year-old boy that provides its own clear window into the nature of men. This story comes out of another lifetime, the one and only year I taught first grade and long before I gave birth to a boy (which is its own tutorial in understanding men). Simply put, I was pretty green.

One day, amid the chaos of a lunchroom of happy children feeling their oats, a small, dark-haired boy came up to me in tears. "What's the problem?" I asked, as I tried to get the rest of the squirming six-year-olds in line.

"A bean is stuck up my nose!" he exclaimed, his eyes wide with panic.

Clearly, he thought I could remedy this problem. Stalling for time, I asked him a second question, equally useless.

"Exactly what possessed you to put a bean up your nose?"

I do not recall how that bean was removed—or perhaps I've blocked it from memory. But today I would no longer need to ask a boy that question. I know, with profound appreciation, the answer. A boy puts a bean up his nose *because he can.*

That very inclination to do something because, after all, it can be done is the way his mind works.

> *A propensity for doing, because it needs to be done and can be done, is the best of who a man is.*

The *drive to do* is quintessentially male. It gets translated the entire length of a guy's life into inventions, achievement, conceptual systems, brick walls and tall glass towers, the New York skyline, and a walk on the moon. A propensity for doing, because it needs to be done and can be done, is the best of who a man is.

It's also one very good part of what he's meant to bring into your life.

We should admit, at the outset, that "what a man does" is a loaded topic these days. What he does is rarely named and seldom heralded. It's not politically correct to blow a trumpet about what men do, unless you want to talk about loud burps or Super Bowl feats. Lots of us have little idea what to expect out of a man, simply because he is a man.

A woman can be eminently successful, known for her own competence and talent. Many doors may have opened to her in her career field. But personal relationships with men largely depend on a different kind of ability, a special sort of insight. A deeper understanding of what God uniquely equips a man to do in life is one of the most important internal perspectives you carry inside you.

> *A woman must be able to see what a man uniquely does— what he's meant to do in this world and in her life—or they both lose out.*

A woman must be able to see what a man uniquely does—what he's meant to do in this world and in her life—or they both lose out.

WHAT'S BEHIND THIS DRIVE

I have observed for years now, with equal parts wonder and frustration, just how given to doing men actually are. Only when I immersed myself in the more recent findings on men's and women's brains did I start to understand what I saw.

Follow me down this trail, because it leads to important things—things that shape your life with men day after day. The men in your world do not have the same brain you have. (You suspected that, right?) Their amygdala tends to be much larger, with far more neurons devoted to action and aggression. Two and half times the space in a man's brain is devoted to sex—which surprises no woman I know. This is simply another way of saying that a man's brain is built for action. Initiative. Energy. Drive. Fire in the belly. Men are made to make things happen. This even has a fancy name in academic circles: "the instrumentality of the male."

Add to this the effect of testosterone. The average guy has forty to sixty times more testosterone floating through his body than you do. No wonder he thinks about sex so often.

During a guy's teen years, his brain gets marinated in testosterone. While this accounts for his renowned interest in all things sexual, it actually causes him to talk and socialize less. Can you imagine? A man's hormones cost him speech. Given that most of us wish the men in our lives talked *more*, it's sobering to think his hormones delete any of those precious words. But they do.

If we add up the neurological picture on simple or sophisticated levels, we can only infer that God actually means for a man's contribution to be what it is—yes, indeed, *doing*. Great things sometimes begin with a bean up the nose . . . so to speak.

Where does this drive to "do" take a man? It generally takes him in the direction of what he instinctively values: action, truth, competence, creative expression, risk taking, initiative, competition, justice, power. That makes sense when we remember that a man was put on the planet to make the earth an inhabitable garden, where everything and everyone in it thrived.[1]

Think of a man you know—or the man in your life—on one of his better days. When he steps out there and does something that takes guts, doesn't something in you want to stand up and applaud? And when he shrinks back, when he hides his strength—don't you feel a sense of loss? *Something is not right here. Where has he gone?*

Those feelings are instinctual evidence of what a man is meant to do and be.

I remember one young woman, newly married, whose banker husband lost his job because of an ethics stand, not long after their wedding. For six months, her income had supported the two of them. She noted that it had been a surprisingly good time.

"Oh, really?" I asked her. "How so?"

"Well, he's always been afraid of losing a job. So blowing the whistle on questionable accounting was really hard for him. My respect for him has grown as I see him confronting his worst fear."

Similarly, I talked with a guy recently who was bemoaning how much his fear of conflict had cost him, in his job and in relationships. It just always seemed easier in the moment to run from the fray. "But how do you feel later?" I asked him, honestly wondering. I was unprepared for the word that came out of his mouth.

"Emasculated. I feel emasculated," he said.

I should not have been surprised. The theme of truth and courage emerges over and over as you talk to men. Something deep in them knows they're meant to expose and speak and fight for what's true—even when it's costly or uncomfortable. And when a man shrinks back from that, he actually feels like less of a man.

Why, one has to ask, would God give men such a bead on truth? Why would he create them with this drive to make something happen? Why does he invest power—a kind of authority of being—in a man? The simple and complicated answer is embodied in two words: *for others*. A man is meant to use his power to create and initiate and build and bless the lives of others. His strength is designed to beat back some of the violence and greed that makes this world a heap of weeds instead of the garden God tried to give us.

> *God invests power and strength in a man for a reason. The question is, how, throughout his life, will he use that power?*

So, of course, it's right for you to expect something in relationships with men. God invests power and strength in a man for a reason. The question is, how, throughout his life, will he use that power?

We know, as women, how ugly it gets when a man abuses his power. It's an old, old story retold in every generation. A man can become a little Herod, insecure and ego driven, chasing down anyone who might possibly take his place. Or he can live like Samson, who surrenders his strength to attractive women, confining his virility to the four corners of a bed when—literally—it was meant to change the world. There are some sad mutations of male power out there.

But it's a huge relational mistake to throw the baby out with the bathwater.

We need an even deeper understanding of the rightness of a man's drive to do. Indeed, the great task of his life is to step into his strength and allow God to use that strength on behalf of others.

Proverbs 31:2-9 provides the most important characteristics of a good man. There are two kinds of men we are warned to steer clear of: the guy who goes from woman to woman, never satisfied, and the man who has been captured by an addiction. (Maybe that sounds obvious, but as most women realize, in real life it's harder than it appears to sort the winners from the losers).

But the third characteristic is key to understanding where God means for a man's talents and his drive to do to take him. Look at this instruction to a man: "Open your mouth, judge righteously, and defend the nights of the afflicted and needy: (Proverbs 31:9).

So God doesn't give a man this "drive to do" so he can pile up a bigger bank account or feel like he's king of the hill. To be a man is to grasp a vision larger than himself.

A MAN'S ABILITY TO DO IS WHAT HE CALLS WORK

The "normal" setting on a man's psyche, then, is task and mission—in short, doing something. What does this mean as you relate to the men in your life, and especially, as you long for a meaningful relationship with one in particular?

In exploring that question, I've tried to let the men I know teach me about their world. Being in the small, cramped space of a counseling office places me in an enviable position because men appear there regularly, ready to talk. As you can imagine, I try to begin on their territory; so I usually ask a guy, quite simply, "What do you do?"

Then I sit back and watch. When you ask a man about his work, he sits up straighter. His face gets more animated, more alive. He engages. I am genuinely curious about how a man navigates his world, so I actually want to know more. How did he get into this line of work? What does he like about it—or why is he itching to do something else? If you have the luxury of just sitting back and watching, you see how much a man enjoys the fact that someone takes seriously what he does out there every day.

And, other than sex, *what he does out there every day* is his most accessible experience of being a man.

As you can also imagine, such nimble curiosity is harder to come by with the man I've been married to for thirty-five years. I *think* I already know all about what Stacy does as a leadership developer and missions leader. I know the challenges he faces—or I think I do. It's easy to let go of the inquisitiveness that lets me wonder and explore with my man—and instead just assume and presume. And when I do, I miss out on a world of stuff swirling inside his head and heart, and we both lose. I have to ask God to help me see, really *see*, the way Stacy feels about the task, the mission—the work—that's so important to him.

A man longs for a few people in his life—most notably, the woman he loves—to get what he's up against every day. There is always someone else (often, the person he's mentoring) who stands ready to take his place—someone who is faster, stronger, and younger. When he fails in any way, it feels public. Or to quote the famous baseball line, "No one wants to strike out in Dodger Stadium, because it's a long way to the dugout." You can talk to ten men in any field, and eight of them will say that work feels just like that to them. There are a hundred eyes watching to see if they blow it and only a precious few who will ever say, "Good job, buddy."

> *A man longs for a few people in his life—most notably, the woman he loves—to get what he's up against every day.*

Knowing that—understanding that—makes me want to be sure that my voice is one that offers a genuine note of respect for the work a man does, however ordinary that might appear.

Listen in, for a moment, on a conversation with a friend as she explained how she began to appreciate the challenges her husband faced in his work. "I used to think of myself as competing with my husband's job," she began. She resented the passion he put into his work. It was time away from her and the kids.

Then she went to work for him in his trucking business. She had her own set of stuff to get done—or something would fall through the cracks. She was the one staying late at the office. "It was one of the best things that ever happened to me," she explained. "I never got, until then, that my husband actually had to put something aside every day to come home."

It's easy to take for granted what a man does—to treat his work like it's old hat.

I guarantee that's not the way a man feels about his job, though. To listen to a man is to hear the steady refrain of the responsibility he carries around. Indeed, one of the major ways a guy grows up on the inside is to feel the weight of other people's lives resting on his shoulders. Little people in padded feet at home need for him to pound the pavement every day. The work a man does is what reminds him on a daily basis that God equips and calls him to exercise his strength on behalf of others.

> *The work a man does is what reminds him on a daily basis that God equips and calls him to exercise his strength on behalf of others.*

The more a woman understands that, the easier it is to ask a man to apply some of that energy toward the finer intricacies of close relationships—where courage and initiative are, also, desperately needed.

THE DRIVE TO DO . . .
AND RELATIONSHIPS

The reality that a man is wired for task—for doing—has important implications for the ways we interpret love. As you can guess, a man expresses love more often by action than by words.

If you ask a random sampling of men how they express love, you will usually get responses like these:

- "Every day I get up and go to a job that requires a lot out of me."

- "I built a deck off the back of the house we could all enjoy."

- "I keep up with the big picture of our finances and try to plan for the future."

- "I turned down a promotion so we could remain close to family."

Another thing a man deeply believes but would not be quick to say is that when he climbs into bed with a woman, he is talking the language of love in the most tangible way possible. Again, a man is far more likely to express what he feels in what he does.

These two differing love languages can be a real challenge when you find yourself starved for a man to say, "Honey, I understand. I get where you're coming from."

Sometimes we ache to hear reassuring words from a man. And he keeps handing us the product, the evidence of what he *does.*

The question many women face is this: *Am I going to count love as it comes to me in a male package? Or am I going to spend my life insisting love be delivered in the manner I recognize most quickly—words and empathy?*

> *The question many women face is this:* Am I going to count love as it comes to me in a male package?

One particularly busy week, when there were too many things coming at me at once, I got in my car and noticed something strange. It was clean. I got out and rubbed my fingers across the door. *Hey, no dust.* Stacy had taken my car to get it washed and cleaned. The dirty truth, though, is that I view cars as small houses on wheels, designed to carry anything I need in a pinch, and having a clean one is not high on my priority list.

I stopped moving so fast on the inside and paid attention. This clean car was a tangible, wordless expression of caring from a man, who, like most men, is far more given to acting on love than talking about it. And I wrapped my arms around his clean-shaven neck and said, "Thank you."

Most men actually have to acquire a spoken language of love. It's a skill they learn over time—something that's hidden in the fine print of relationships. Words seem so obvious. But to most men, they are far harder to access. Their private grief is that what they do, out of love, often doesn't seem to register to a woman in a way she translates as feeling loved.

LETTING UNDERSTANDING
LEAD YOU SOMEWHERE

The longer you live with a man, the more it strikes you that God might actually be trying to say something about our nature—our essence—through our physical differences.

Sometimes, I get the feeling that sexual intimacy is a type of Braille where the subject being read is, actually, the soul.

Might there be meaning, for example, to the reality that God gives a man broader shoulders than you? Isn't there some invitation in that to lean your weight on him, at least when you need to? Or think of all the muscle mass in a man's body. Surely that is present for a purpose—as though this guy is truly meant to do something in the world.

There are a hundred physical analogies to be drawn, nearly all embedded with meaning. The most celebrated part of a man's anatomy is both sensitive and strong; its penetration quite literally brings life. In the act of intimacy, a woman receives the strength a man brings—strength she cannot replicate on her own. There are lots of clues to the soul hidden in the common simplicity of a man and woman coming together.

I think our bodies act out the mystery of who we are in

ways our conscious minds can't quite absorb. *This man is not like me. And I am not like him.* And, somehow, if I listen to that—if I pay attention—what dawns on me is a much deeper appreciation for a man's maleness. God created two genders because the beauty and power of his nature cannot be expressed in this world by anything less.

What I hope to carry with me all my life from that understanding is just a little bit of awe.

This understanding about what God uniquely equips a man to do in life—and especially, in our lives—is like a wise, intuitive knowing that shapes how we relate to him. It gives us an ability to hold back a bit and invite his strength to emerge. We are better able to appreciate the ways he expresses love in a particularly male manner. Our longing for a man to act like a man is not something we are ashamed to own.

> *God created two genders because the beauty and power of his nature cannot be expressed in this world by anything less.*

But, and this is a big *but*, the more you realize that a man is called to a place of strength and courage, the wilder your roller-coaster ride in relationships may be. It begs the question: what do you do with the disappointment you feel when a man fails you? Where do you turn when you can't get the empathy and support you long for? How do you cope when a man runs away from the challenge of a close relationship and you feel left in the dust?

It's easy to internally dispense with a man (or to write off men in general) because you have wanted something he has not been able or willing to give—or at least, not yet. Maybe he hasn't grown to that point. Perhaps he never will. In many ways, this book is about dealing with that disappointment in ways that don't stomp on your heart—or his.

> *The more you realize that a man is called to a place of strength and courage, the wilder your roller-coaster ride in relationships may be.*

It is indeed a bigger challenge to hold your heart open to the hope that this man will realize a strength that is genuinely his, strength you can count on in tough moments. Disappointment will be embedded in that journey. But the starting point is understanding more about what makes a man . . . a man.

Chapter 3

WHY MEN HURT

Ever since man emerged from the dominance of nature, masculinity has been the most fragile and problematic of psychic states.
—CAMILLE PAGLIA

It's easy to be snowed by the way a man looks. Those broad shoulders, the confident smile, the way he moves from his BlackBerry to his son's basketball game. Who would guess there are issues rumbling beneath the surface in which he feels pain—or something like pain?

Half the time he hardly knows that himself.

A guy reveals precious little vulnerability in his relationships. I know this is true for reasons I hate to admit: I listen in on their conversations. It's an ability I've perfected over time to a fine art. And while I trust you are above the temptation, it provides me with a steady supply of wonder. It also confirms a few insights that could not be gathered easily in other ways.

Dozens of conversations among men sound just like the one I overheard recently at a coffee shop deep in the North Carolina mountains. Here were three guys who'd clearly been friends awhile, happy to be together, bear hugs all around.

What fascinating things did they discuss? What caused them to set aside this date so they could be in each other's company?

I'm almost embarrassed to say. The conversation progressed from small talk about plans for the week to larger, more important matters like . . . how the next football season is shaping up. And how much traveling one guy was doing for his job. And what was left on that remodeling project the other guy was finishing. That's it. The conversation I overheard, one they sure seemed to enjoy, would bore five pounds off most women I know.

Now, I have no doubt these guys enjoyed the time. If I'd stuck a microphone in their faces, they would have said, "Hey, it was great!" Some special kind of strength and support is exchanged between men in such times—invisibly, as they simply hang out together.[1] Somewhere in my head, I know that. But I'm still amazed.

Women require more. It's not that our conversations are more enlightened, but if we gather as friends, you can bet that someone will put her feelings into words, sooner or later. Someone will ask how your alcoholic sister is doing—discreetly, but she'll ask. You'll voice your support for this new, high-pressure job your friend is taking. Vulnerability is rewarded among women—if you call these women "friends." Strokes of support are more obvious. It's the reason you do lunch.[2]

The sheer contrast of those two pictures explains something about why the man in your life may see you as his safest relationship. Men don't collaborate with each other as much as they compete. You may be the only person who knows where the cracks in his armor are. It's not your responsibility to heal the hurt in his life, but understanding what he fears does present a great opportunity for you both.

Understanding the hidden vulnerabilities of any man you know will provide important clues in how you relate well to men.

MORE REASONS TO BE GLAD YOU'RE A WOMAN

So let's look past his cool, bemused gaze. What's he really thinking? Or more specifically, what are the weights a man carries, the sore places in his psyche, even if he doesn't talk about them easily?

One fundamental reality is that a man lives with a challenging combination of great expectations amid great isolation. *Hunter, gatherer, father, warrior, husband, brother—but don't let anyone see you sweat.* That's always been a man's mandate. These days he may try to dispense with the husband and father part. But the men you're around know they need to slay dragons of some sort. He's got to stand up and be a man—or risk hating himself to his last breath.

> *It's not your responsibility to heal the hurt in his life, but understanding what he fears does present a great opportunity for you both.*

To this ancient prescription a relatively new requirement has been added: he must be somewhat proficient in "doing relationships." No more sitting in stoic silence—the modern guy needs to be sensitive, insightful, and caring. That's all fine and great, but the sheer biology presents a few challenges. A woman's brain is far more equipped to interpret facial expression, tone of voice, and unspoken messages.[3] So you might say that relationally, more is required of a man—but, neurologically, he's underequipped.

THE FEMALE BRAIN

The female brain has its own bells and whistles. Your hippocampus is larger than a man's. Its elaborate circuitry accounts for your ability from birth to watch faces and maintain eye contact.

By the time a baby girl is three months old, her people skills have increased 400 percent, while a boy's have stayed nearly the same. This head start, then, molds brain circuitry as a girl gets rewarded by all those smiling faces. She learns what those expressions mean. Before long, she has far outpaced her male counterparts in this ability.

What's more, during the first two years of your life (and again in your teens), your brain was bathed in estrogen—increasing your already sizable ability to tune in to people and to express empathy with words. To what end is this amazing design? Louann Brizendine, the neuropsychiatrist who authored *The Female Brain*, writes, "Why is a girl born with such a highly tuned machine for reading faces, hearing emotional tones in voices, and responding to unspoken cues in others? Think about it. A machine like that is built for connection. That's the main job of the girl brain, and that's what [drives a female from birth]."[4]

Sometimes a good novelist can put words to the difference in men and women and, particularly, the pressure a man feels. Listen to Elizabeth Berg as she cuts to the chase:

I have a personal theory about why most men walk away from difficult situations: It's because they don't have babies. It is bred in them to leave the dwelling place to hunt and gather, to be outward-oriented; it is bred in women to lie down and give birth and stay home in order to care for the small world they have delivered into the larger one. Men conk things on the head or are conked themselves; women work out the kinks of the inner life.[5]

"Men conk things on the head or are conked themselves." That's not exactly why I get out of bed in the mornings. But

I believe that if you listen well to men, those words express, in some deeply primal way, the challenge a man is up against—one he feels uniquely and in the deepest fibers of his being. He doggone better go after things before they come after him. The lives of other people will rise or fall based on his resourcefulness. This is the inner awareness God puts in men.

IS HE MAN ENOUGH?

Lurking beneath every conversation you have with a man is this theme of adequacy. Is he enough of a man—for this job, these children, this whatever? And most especially, is he man enough to merit your respect?[6] It's the unspoken measuring stick in every encounter you have with a man.

There are good reasons for this. Women establish a psychological identity easier than men do because our bodies tell us more intrinsically who we are. You walk around in a body that can actually house people. You

> *Lurking beneath every conversation you have with a man is this theme of adequacy. Is he enough of a man— for this job, these children, this whatever?*

can keep another person alive for an entire year on the nourishment you alone produce. There is a beauty and attraction in your femaleness that a man desires, and apart from rape, you become the one who chooses whether his overtures will be received. For these reasons and more, many would argue that women hold a "sexually superior" position.[7]

I bet you don't feel all that superior, though. I would never have thought in those terms, as a woman, because I didn't get the vulnerability men feel about their sexuality. I can find myself feeling impatient with men: Why do they need to prove their masculinity? Why can't a man just *be* as confident as he *looks*? What is going on?

I can only understand when I begin on the level of the physical. The most fundamental clues to men, both psychologically and spiritually, are discovered in their sexual being. Men live with a sexual predicament that colors their whole experience of life. A man's body has only one expression of being male—and that's intercourse. And in that sexual act, a man, unlike a woman, must perform. Nothing happens unless he performs. As author George Gilder insightfully writes, "[A] man is less secure sexually than [a] woman because his sexuality is dependent on action, and he can act sexually only through a process difficult to control. . . . Nothing comes to them by waiting or 'being.' For men the desire for sex is not simply a quest for pleasure. It is an indispensable test of identity."[8]

Is it any wonder, then, that whether it's on the job or just bringing you flowers, a man usually weighs himself on the basis of performance? Being a man is more like a prize that must be won, if he can—always and only, if he can. If he's enough of a man.[9]

If feeling adequate is a man's Achilles' heel, then you can understand why the kind of vulnerability that allows others to see his weaknesses or flaws can feel about as crazy to him as jumping off a cliff with holes in his parachute. It makes sense why taking any sort of initiative with you, especially, feels riskier than you might think. Or as a man would express his most primal fear: *If I stick it out there, she may lob it off.* (Pardon the earthy metaphor.)[10]

HOW GOD SPEAKS INTO A MAN'S SEXUALITY

In a man's life, the driving force in his personal and spiritual development is his sexuality. It's the way God designed him. The mystery of his being is there. And for this reason, in a guy's secret life, he will admit that his triumphal moments and his worst wounds both find their source here.

> *In a man's life, the driving force in his personal and spiritual development is his sexuality.*

You know, perhaps, how women talk about the actual experience of sex. It's an odd mix of great fun and a necessity for producing a child. It's a refuge from a long day—or maybe, just one more thing to check off a mental list. But your sense of worth and identity is rarely hanging in the balance. Women have little, well-decorated compartments in their brains, and the one with bold colors is labeled "sex." They don't live there; they just go there, on occasion.

A man has a far more seamless psyche. So everything about his sexuality is connected: meeting his sales quota, teaching on his favorite subject, throwing baseballs. It's all-of-a-piece. I know if I live to be a hundred, I will never fully get the way a man feels about the experience of sex.[11] But I have read enough and heard enough to sense that, for a man, sex is some kind of direct pipeline of validation—a recurring confirmation that he has what it takes to face the world.

It's so potent, in fact, that a man's lifelong temptation is to turn sex into a god and to make you (or some other woman) the center of his universe, rather than a person and a partner.

I stand in awe of the way God steps into the center of this drama in a man's life, from the beginning. Think of the rite of circumcision. God's intervention into a pagan, hedonistic culture came in an act in which a Hebrew boy's very flesh was cut. From his earliest days, a man's sexuality was marked by the touch of God on his life. Daily he had the most graphic reminder possible that his sexuality was, first of all, a matter of covenant between God and him. When he saw his own flesh, he remembered to whom he belonged.

This theme follows man throughout Scripture. His sexuality is a wild, creative power in his life—but it cannot be allowed to rule. In celibacy before marriage and faithfulness to one woman, a man submits to God the most potent force in. And God, who is no man's debtor, provides the richest dividends of his life: children, family, deep connection to others, posterity. He becomes not less of a man, bound by restriction, but more of the man God created him to be. He steps into an even fuller experience of the man he actually is.

Yes, in the arena of his sexuality, radical business is done in a man's heart between him and God. The paradox is that men usually don't do that sort of business without feeling pain.

WHEN THE TWO OF YOU ARE NOT ENOUGH

Unprocessed pain in a man's life can spill over in destructive ways in a relationship. It's important to know when you should seek help from some third party—be that a pastor, counselor, or doctor. Here are a few things that should not be overlooked:

- When a man's lack of initiative, irritability, or hopelessness may be a symptom of depression—he needs medical help and someone to talk to about the issues in his life

- When you express a reasonable need and he repeatedly interprets that as an effort to control him

- When anger is the primary form his pain takes

- When his chosen form of escape is pornography or substance abuse[12]

- When you are the only person in the relationship who can be at fault
- When there's a pattern of repeating childhood drama in your present relationship and you repeatedly sense that he (or you) are shadowboxing with the past

In these situations, the sooner you get help, the easier it is to make substantive change.

A QUESTION ONLY GOD CAN ANSWER

A man's sexuality is the place in his life where, often, he hurts the most. And if he follows that pain like bread crumbs left on a trail, it leads somewhere quite wonderful. I offer this man's camouflaged story as one among many.

> *A man's sexuality is the place in his life where, often, he hurts the most.*

Fred was an engineer who never thought his wife would cheat on him. Never. And I'm not sure you could call what she did cheating—not exactly. She got emotionally involved with a man who played second violin to her first violin in a local symphony. With Fred's knowledge, they began to meet for lunch, innocently enough at first, two insiders planning for future musical events. But Mr. Second Violin was lonely after his wife left him, and before long, he began to reach across the table to hold her hand. That made her a little nervous, but she enjoyed the conversations so much she ignored it. The day he kissed her as they parted, she woke up. She had a guilty little secret on her hands.

Like it or not, she had to tell Fred. She knew if she could just tell him the truth, most of this would disappear in the stark light of honesty. And while she would miss the music conversations with the guy who played second violin, Fred was her husband. About that, she was clear.

She was unprepared for Fred's reaction. The idea that his wife had been attracted to another man—that she could have ended up in bed with him—was a blow to the gut. It unearthed every insecurity he'd stuffed for twenty years, all the locker-room banter about who was most endowed, his misgivings about why he wanted sex twice as often as his wife.

In our counseling sessions, Fred kept trying to make his pain his wife's issue. "I don't think I can ever trust her again," he would complain, as though her very character was tainted beyond repair.

"Your wife is going to come through this fine," I reassured him. "Your marriage can be better than it ever was."

The issue was really how Fred felt about Fred. "How are you going to let your wife's mistake be her mistake and not some commentary on you as a man?" I asked him.

Whether a guy confronts this question through a battle

with pornography or someone's infidelity or feeling like his wife is not good enough in bed, the question is nearly always the same: *who and what has the power to make him a real man?*

That question cannot be answered adequately by the woman in a man's life. Or as John Eldredge says so well in his book *Wild at Heart*,

> . . . femininity can never bestow masculinity. It's like asking a pearl to give you a buffalo. It's like asking a field of wildflowers to give you a '57 Chevy. They are different substances entirely.
>
> When a man takes his question to the woman what happens is either addiction or emasculation. Usually both.[13]

So, for a man, the deep question of his life is one that only God can answer. Only God.

Only the one who made him, who loaned him a piece of his own strength and authority and shaped his very body to reflect his masculine soul.

A man cannot earn his validation. He can only claim it as a gift God bestows. That can be the greatest realization of his life.

THE HUMAN VOICE THAT MATTERS

There's one other sore place in a man's psyche with a particular sort of vulnerability. Let's follow this through Fred's story.

As Fred began to ask him-
self why he felt so devastated
by his wife's betrayal, the trail
of bread crumbs led back into
his life growing up. When Fred
was eight years old, his older
brother broke his arm playing

> *Standing off on the side
> of a man's mind is one
> figure that towers above
> all others: Dad.*

baseball. The doctor ran a few tests and discovered that his
bone shattered for other reasons. For the next two years, Fred
watched as his family desperately tried to save his brother
from bone cancer. After he died, his dad was so deep in grief
for the next few years that, as Fred says, "he hardly knew I
was still there." Fred plowed his own path through adolescence
and out into the bigger world.

Standing off on the side of a man's mind is one figure that
towers above all others: *Dad*. The very word carries special
weight. His father's voice is the holy voice, humanly speaking.

If a man had a good-enough father, then he feels there is
some sort of wind in his sails to carry him through stormy
seas. Or to change the metaphor, his father is always out ahead
of him on the path. There is, at least, the faint trail of footsteps
to follow. It is his attitude of acceptance that matters most.

As Frank Pittman writes in his book *Man Enough*, "Our
father . . . has the authority to let us relax the requirements of
the masculine model: if our father accepts us, then that declares
us masculine enough to join the company of men. We, in effect,
have our diploma in masculinity and can go on to develop
other skills."[14]

If a guy's father left him—by abandonment or adultery or a trauma like grief—then a hole exists inside him that's big enough to drive a truck through. Good things, like his sexuality, come to mean more than they are meant to. He can easily fall prey to the bondage of believing that some external something—be it a woman or a red convertible or the corner office—will fully baptize him as a man.

Of course, the fly in the ointment between sons and their fathers is that every son longs to hear his father tell him what a fantastic guy he is. But as you already know, words between men are often in short supply. I will never forget a friend sharing with me the terrific irony of his dad's funeral. Right before he got in the funeral car headed to the cemetery, his dad's good friend came up to him and patted him on the back. "You know, your dad was always so proud of you," he said.

All his life, my friend had waited, in vain, to hear those words from his dad's mouth. Here was his father's friend voicing them on the day his father was being buried.

I take special note of the sweet sacredness of the moment in Jesus' life when, out of the blue, his Father spoke in audible words everyone could hear: "This is My beloved Son, in whom I am well-pleased."[15] The Father claimed the Son as his own and told him and everyone listening just how happy with him he was. You can think forever about the secret longings of your own heart, and they will boil down to this: the desire to belong, deeply, to someone who is pleased with you. God is the Father we have always, always, always wanted.

But let's return to this thing of fathers-in-the-flesh.

Apparently, God mirrors a different sort of love through a father than he does through a mother. A mother's love is assumed, taken for granted. *Of course, your mother loves you. That's what mothers do.*

But your father stands at a greater distance. His love is not a given. His love feels like a choice. He chooses you, notices you from among the many—much like God chose Israel as a nation to display his love and affection. "The LORD did not set His love on you nor choose you because you were more in number than any of the peoples, for you were the fewest of all peoples, but because the LORD loved you."[16]

That is the uniquely transformative experience of male love. "It validates us and affirms us deeply, precisely because it is not necessary. It is totally free love, non-needy, non-manipulative, non-codependent—and only such love finally feels like love at all. Of course, a good mother loves in that way, too."[17]

It seems that God gives fathers a special voice inside our heads—and this is even more true for a man.

A guy's father is also a walking road map into the world of men. He learns by watching, by doing, and occasionally, even by a bit of verbal instruction. Mostly it's just absorbed through the air between them, like sheer instinct.

> *It seems that God gives fathers a special voice inside our heads—and this is even more true for a man.*

When our son turned fourteen, I remember noticing that my husband seemed lost in relating to him. Then, it struck me one day: that's the age when his own father left for California and never returned. So Stacy (who has been, by the grace of God, quite a good dad) found that he had no internal map, at that point, for what a dad does with his son. "I feel like a walk-on—like I have to make it up as I go along," he would say. The footsteps on the trail ahead of him had disappeared inside.

Occasionally, men do actually take each other by the shoulders and give direct advice. My favorite piece of that comes out of Texas, from a friend who was given, on occasion, to emotional meltdowns. She knew she would recover, but only after she'd gone through a box of Kleenex. One day she overheard her husband tell their teenage son, "Look, this is what you do when this kind of thing happens: you hold a woman and let her cry and tell her you love her . . . and then you carefully back up ten feet and give her some space."

It's really not bad advice.

HIS STORY IS THE KEY TO HIS HEART

Understanding a bit about the vulnerability in a man's sexuality and how his father influenced his life is really just the prologue and the preamble. You can't really know a man until you know his story. Not just the facts—but the whole story, as if you lived there awhile and absorbed the feelings he might not have words for.

Fred's wife, for example, always wondered what drove him so hard. Why did he run perpetually late, usually putting in twice the effort that a job required? Where did his heavy sense of responsibility come from?

When you begin to walk around in another person's story, it's like watching snapshots being slowly developed. Fuzzy images become clearer. Fred's wife could finally see a ten-year-old boy who lost his brother—and then his father—in one tragic season. The guilt of being the son who survived, the pressure to make good, the fear that someone would discover him as an imposter—she began to feel some of what Fred felt.

Let me be clear that Fred was the only one who could deal with the emotional baggage he was carrying. But what a difference it makes when two people can talk about it. Fears have a way of shrinking as you name them—and especially as you pray about them. The lies you believed in the painful parts of your story start to lose their grip. And mysteriously—almost magically—you realize that the problem is *not* the other person.

Not really.

I am convinced that in any personal relationship with a man, be it husband or brother or son or father, you will never feel close to him until you can feel the impact of the story he's lived. And everyone has a story. Everyone.

If you keep adding to the collection of mental snapshots that help you feel the impact of the stories that the important men in your life have lived, you'll find they give you insight in crucial moments.

How about that scene of your husband, as a boy, sitting on the front porch, watching his dad's car pull out for the last time, knowing his world would never be the same? Maybe this new job you've been offered takes him back to the same fear and paralysis he experienced in the face of change.

Or think of your demanding brother-in-law. Can you picture him at age ten as his mom, martini in hand, tells him to stay in his room all day because he hasn't made his bed well enough? Perhaps his disparaging remark about how your children behave reflects more about how he feels about himself than what he thinks of you or your kids.

This collection of snapshots grows larger as time goes by. I knew, for example, that when Stacy's dad took a job in California, it was a painful chapter of his past. Only when I attended a later high school reunion did I realize that, in the suburbs of Columbus, Ohio, in 1966, no one Stacy knew had parents filing for divorce. I was shocked. Suddenly, the shame of that divorce was something I could feel.

> *The reason you try to understand where a man hurts is not because it's your job to fix or heal him. That would be impossible.*

When my father was declining as an old man and, in many ways, pulling his life apart with his own hands, I found myself returning to his story. One scene, in particular, kept coming to mind: my father as a twenty-one-year-old man, standing beside the wreck of an old Pontiac as the bodies of his mother and his older sister and her child were carried away on stretchers. My father was driving the car that day. It was sad he was falling apart as an old man. But it was a small miracle he'd made it that far. Without that mental picture, I might have lost the relationship I had with him.

SAVING GRACE

I don't want to leave you with the wrong impression. The reason you try to understand where a man hurts is not because it's your job to fix or heal him. That would be impossible. God does not lay that responsibility on you. Living under that delusion could pose disaster for you both.

No, insight shapes perspective. And perspective influences the quality of your relationship. Here are a few places where more insight can take you:

- *Respect for this man's particular challenges.* If you understand his vulnerabilities, you have far more appreciation for the times when he exercises risk and courage.

- *A patience that does not excuse.* Your understanding of his story does not whitewash bad behavior. Your insight doesn't just overlook his short-comings. No matter what has happened in his life, God puts strength at the core of his being. So you

can be patient with this man without erasing your
expectations of him.

- *An antidote for taking things too personally.* If you
  can read a man's vulnerabilities, then when he's
  irritable or withdrawn, it's easier to see clearly.
  This might well have little to do with you. It's
  more about him and the way he chooses to meet
  the challenges of his life. Then it's possible to ask
  things like, "What's bothering you? You don't
  seem like yourself."

- *Awareness of how much your support matters.* When
  you can see a man's struggle with adequacy, your
  affirmation (or lack of) takes on real meaning. It's
  not the ultimate answer, but it's truly important.

- *Dialogue about your own struggles and losses.*
  Understanding where a man hurts is a window
  into helping him make sense of the pain you feel
  and why you need for him to "be there" for you in
  certain ways. For example, "Remember how you
  felt when you weren't accepted to medical school?
  I feel a similar kind of loss when . . ."

The goal is not to heal the other person, because, truly,
that is a work only God can do as the saving power of Christ
invades the dark, hidden places of our hearts. But in close relationships, we live to see that redemption take place.[18] Mostly,
we're along for the ride. Occasionally, when we are least

aware, God actually uses us in the process.

Being a woman who understands a man—perhaps better than he understands himself—will allow you to see beyond his fears or defeats. Only God can really meet him. But it's a gift when you can see there's a man in there, in spite of everything.

> *Being a woman who understands a man— perhaps better than he understands himself— will allow you to see beyond his fears or defeats.*

It's a gift, even though you know that, ultimately, he has to claim that reality for himself.

Chapter 4

HOW MEN CHANGE

Why won't he be the king I know he is, the king I see inside?
—"CAN YOU FEEL THE LOVE TONIGHT?"
FROM *THE LION KING*

A friend called just as I was beginning this chapter: "*What part* of this saga about men are you writing these days?" she asked.

I told her I was writing about how men change.

"Oh, really," she said. And then she added, "Do you think men change?"

I think I understand her response. Men do change, of course. But the process is so different from a woman's experience that sometimes you wonder. A man might be quite depressed, and hardly anyone will know. He might rethink his whole life, and the only clue would be a quick, sudden decision no one saw coming.

It's easy to miss that profound things can be shifting inside a man. Just because his manner of change is less visible and accompanied by less fanfare, doesn't mean nothing's happening. Not by a long shot.

HOW WOULD YOU KNOW?

I remember watching a woman named Alice spend hours explaining to her husband the subtle nuances of why their relationship wasn't working very well. He listened for a long time without saying much. You had to wonder if her comments were falling into some abyss. Was he getting it?

One day, out of the blue, he summarized their problem. "You nag me because I don't do. And I run away from you because I don't want to be nagged."

Once he voiced the problem, of course, it was easier to find a way out. But what struck me then has impressed me countless times: men are often amazingly able to bottom-line an issue. You wonder how they arrive at a particular insight, though, because rarely do they feel the need to talk their way there.

Men simply live less inward lives. They hear a complaint or respond to an

> *Men are often amazingly able to bottom-line an issue.*

emotional event, and it's filed someplace out of sight where their brains distill the important pieces as they sleep or trim shrubbery.

A man may signal change not with words but by making a different choice. He may offer few words and little discussion—he just does things differently.

That's what happened with Alice and her husband. She

had one particular complaint: he expected too much from her with the children and didn't appreciate the sacrifices she was making because he traveled. She wrote him a letter about how much this bothered her, thinking that, surely, he would offer some apology. She thought they would sit down and discuss the matter.

Her husband made few comments about getting her note. But he did cut back on his travel and take a more active role with their children. He genuinely made some changes, but you'd only know that by watching his actions. You would wish he put words to an apology of some sort. But men—even good men—sometimes signal change a different way.

That's why it's important to study the man you love, to notice and praise the subtle shifts in what he does. If you comment on positive changes, it solidifies a new direction. He stands up two inches taller. It matters more to him because it matters to you. We all tend to rise to the level of someone else's positive expectation.

TASTING DEFEAT

So men change by less perceptible means. And often, men don't change much without encountering crisis or defeat. That's the plain truth of the matter. It's a theme you hear repeated in the lives of guys who've grown into men of stature and maturity.

It's natural, as a woman, to want a man to step from one

glowing success to the next. It's scary when his plans don't pan out. You can lose sleep worrying about how he will handle what he alone may see as failure. But the best men in the long run learn (as early as possible) that they don't have the world by the tail. They finally get that they're more than the job they do. They stop trying to be a one-man show. They need other people. And they need God. In other words, men learn important things the hard way.

> *Men learn important things the hard way.*

I have a friend whose husband didn't get the leadership job he wanted. He felt he'd been prepared for this role for ten years—and then the door slammed shut. For almost a year, the loss really threw him. "How did you handle an unhappy, struggling man?" I asked my friend. Her answer made me think.

"Somehow, I realized that my husband had to wrestle this disappointment to the ground, and this wasn't going to be an overnight recovery," she said. "And though I knew it wasn't going to be easy for either of us, I could also sense that good things would come of it, and it would be worth the wait."

Oh, wow. That takes phenomenal patience. It takes real insight to see that deep change in a man's life usually occurs paradoxically—meaning, he runs smack into the weakness or failure he's worked so hard to prevent. But this is the way God works in all our lives—and often, even more dramatically, in a man's. Think of David, an unlikely choice for a king, whose character training took place as he hid in caves from a man seeking to kill him.[1] How else could his heart for God be shaped? Or Jacob, conniving his way through life, collecting wives and children and sheep like a desert chieftain. He is a changed man, but only after he has been defeated and has wrestled with something—or Someone—greater than himself.[2]

The best men hit a wall before their hair gets very gray. The earlier the better. A man's deepest fears get burned off as he faces them head-on. A bit more humility serves every future success. It is the process by which he becomes a man of character and integrity.

Understanding that allows a woman to ride out the storm.

THE INFLUENCE OF A WOMAN

There are a few experiences where, when shared in a group of women, you can watch every head nod. Here is one of them. You've been seeing this guy for a couple of years—or maybe you married him. Maybe he's your son. You know you matter to him. You've gently suggested and jokingly inferred that, really, he might want to rethink his approach to something. "Honey, you might want to do that a tad differently." He nods—and changes the subject.

A few months later, he tells you about a conversation with his buddy. An incredible new insight has dawned on him. Lo and behold, his friend made the same suggestion you had made earlier—only now, it strikes him as a brilliant idea, something he should act on very soon.

If you're like me, you fight the urge to reply, "But I said that six months ago."

Like I say, this experience is so universal it's hard to convince women that all through a man's life, God uses his relationship with a woman to shape deep, important things in him. Not because it's your intention—but because it's God's design.

GETTING MARRIED

When you were young, you probably sang the nursery song, "The farmer takes a wife . . ." It sounds like he purchased her at a market in town. But really, the meaning is that he takes on the responsibility of a wife and, eventually, children.

It's an awesome step.

My friend's brother made an insightful comment a few years ago. He said, "A woman dies to herself—to her dreams and her agenda—when she has children. But a similar kind of death happens in a man when he gets married."

In love and courtship and marriage, a man must invest himself on some level that, to him, feels like a sweet death. He knows, deep in his gut, he is taking on the responsibility of others' lives in a whole new

> *All through a man's life, God uses his relationship with a woman to shape deep, important things in him.*

way. Yes, marriage will usher him into family and posterity—someone to have Christmas with when he's sixty. But getting there means giving up his independence. It means narrowing his possibilities for many women down to one. One woman. Marriage, truly, might be the most dramatic change in a man's life.

> *Marriage, truly, might be the most dramatic change in a man's life.*

A guy feels that every step he makes out of the safe, pubescent company of boys into the uncharted territory of females is a long, perilous trek filled with hidden land mines and barbed wire. (Maybe God knew men would need every ounce of that testosterone to keep them moving forward.)

Imagine how you would feel if you had a strong, urgent need for something but no internal map of how to get there. That's a fairly good description of what men face all their lives as their sexuality drives them toward relationship—but relationships are not exactly their forte. What a combination. Courage is required, and courage is something from which no man should be saved. Perhaps some words I wrote in an earlier book would help here:

> Does it strike you what a gift it is to a guy when he has to be the one to pursue you? Men become men by doing battle with their fears, and pursuing a woman well is a

process filled with man-sized risks. He must cross the floor to ask you to dance at thirteen. He picks up the phone later, braced for the sound of rejection or reception in your voice. On and on the dance goes until one day he must gather the courage to stake his whole future on asking you to be his wife.

At every juncture, a man feels naked and exposed, braced for the turndown. But that's the nature of fear; it only subsides when you walk straight into it. To grow up inside a man must get over his fear of Woman. For as we all know, you come to hate the things you fear. How can a man ever love you well if he is so afraid of your rejection?[3]

The first significant shifts in a man's consciousness and his awareness of his impact on others happen only as he grapples with the power of his sexual drive. When a woman rewards his overtures with sex—and he does not have to step into the covenant of marriage to get it—a terribly important process in him is aborted. This is why so many men now stay stuck in adolescent sexuality. *Give me what I need, and don't ask anything of me.* You meet a thirty-five-year-old man, and you have the strangest feeling you are talking to a guy who is eighteen on the inside.

A friend of mine told me recently about a conversation he had on a long flight overseas, seated next to a younger guy from the Middle East who had spent a lot of time in the United States. Midway through dinner this man admitted, "You know,

I love your country. It's so easy to sleep with a woman. Of course, I won't marry until I go back to my country, and she'll be a virgin."

Then with genuine curiosity, the young man asked my friend, "What is it with your culture that women give away their power so easily?"

HELPING HIS HEAD FIND HIS HEART

I don't mean to paint a picture of men as relational klutzes. That's neither fair nor accurate. But I meet many women—and I've been there myself—living under the illusion that what's intuitively obvious to us in a relationship, something we can feel in our bones, must be just as clear to him. So if he doesn't see the obvious, we think he's holding out on us. And we feel hurt.

When all is said and done, there are, roughly, three kinds of men out there. Some are nearly crippled in their ability to line up the dots needed to make close relationships work. They may be alexythymic, meaning they lack the ability to identify what they or others feel. Without the words to express a feeling, they aren't able to own it. Often, and understandably, this kind of man works with machines or in a job removed from the needs of people.[4]

The second, and largest, group of men can line up the dots necessary for relationships, but they rely on insight they gather from others. Often, their best sources are the women in their lives, women like you. You probably supply some missing pieces you don't even know you're supplying, and this sort of man takes them and runs in the right direction. As I say, most men rely on a woman, more than they care to admit, to help them see the hidden reefs in relationships. And what they give in return is, hopefully, a rational, thoughtful objectivity that's profoundly valuable.

Then, at the other end of the spectrum, there's a third group of men in a category all their own. This kind of guy gets it before you do. He not only gets it, but he throws out insights only a man would pick up on. You find yourself taking mental notes when he speaks. This is a small category, though—consisting mostly of poets, therapists, or men who have suffered greatly.

You may have an inadequate appreciation for the role you play in helping a man dance the intricacies of feelings and relationships. Without a close connection to a woman, he can remain a bull in a china shop—or a passive observer who sits out his life.

When you wonder what you naturally pick up in a conversation, consider the implications of these findings:[5]

- Unless there are actual tears present, men can tell another person feels sad only about 40 percent of the time. Women pick up subtler signs of sadness 90 percent of the time. This confirms what you intuitively knew: you came equipped with tear ducts that work for some good reason.

- The term *gut feelings* actually has a physical basis. Studies show that women have significantly more neurons assigned to tracking stomach sensations. So when you know "in your gut" how someone felt or what needed to be said, you are probably more accurate than you realize.

- If a man and a woman are wired to computers and the same sad story is told to them, an average of six times as many neurons will light up in a woman's brain compared to a man's. (Do you ever find yourself wondering why he seems less affected by a loss you're reeling from?)

- Men struggle far harder to interpret facial expressions. And there are changes in voice tone their ears actually do not hear.

- A man's natural tendency is to give people their space when they're going through a rough time. The code of respect among men assumes that a person prefers to process difficult feelings alone. It's a way of saving face. Learning to be with people while they're feeling awful is a skill men most often learn from a woman.

I know there are exceptions to all of this, but they are exceptions. Most guys make internal shifts in the way they do life and relationships because a woman has helped them see what they often can't. A man may not realize he's walked on your heart with cleats until you tell him, or until he sees tears.[6]

For a man, connecting his head with his heart most often happens through a close relationship with a woman, as they are both willing to risk some vulnerability.

SAYING THE RIGHT KIND OF "NO"

I mentioned earlier that men make painful changes in their lives as they bump up against a crisis of some sort. Occasionally, you may be the crisis.

When Tracy and Ed married, Ed was finishing dental school. Not having much money, they lived on love. Nobody could squeeze a dollar better than Ed, though. He paid off his dental practice much sooner than his friends did theirs. But he could not relax. His father lost the family farm, years before, when tobacco went under. In Ed's mind, the words *fear* and *money* always went together.

> *Most guys make internal shifts in the way they do life and relationships because a woman has helped them see what they often can't.*

Strangely enough, Ed could find the funds for his favorite sport—fly-fishing. He took yearly trips to Montana with a tribe of local guys. Tracy didn't have a problem with that. She appreciated that he was, also, a generous giver. What she resented was his frugal approach to her and the kids. Somehow, there was never money in the budget for a trip she wanted to take as a family or remodeling the bathroom.

It's not as if Tracy didn't bring up her desires. But Ed had been a championship debater in college, and he knew how to present his argument well. "Honey, look, I've got a plan for where we need to be in retirement." He'd put her off to the next year. And Tracy would back down. After all, Ed's salary kept them afloat.

Tracy was a sharp woman, though, and she suspected that the real problem was not lack of income but rather Ed's fear related to money. As long as she kept backing down, he wouldn't ever have to deal with his fear.

So Tracy screwed up her nerve and said five words—five very important words. She said them without anger. She said them without putting Ed down. When they got on the subject of a family trip again, Ed said what he usually said. But this time, Tracy replied, "That won't work for me."

"What do you mean that won't work for you?" Ed thought he was hallucinating.

Tracy stuck to her guns—quietly, firmly. "I mean that won't work for me. We have to find a different solution."

The ball was in Ed's court. Finally. If something won't work for someone, it simply won't work. You have to choose another option. You have to come up with plan B.

Ed would tell you that the crisis of finding plan B was what God used to cause him to look at how much his life was driven by fear—especially related to money. He did not fundamentally trust God to provide. Instead, he felt that the family's financial security was entirely up to him, and since he needed fly-fishing to keep going, then the fishing trips felt justified. He found some Bible verses about greed and the wise use of money. And those verses led him to a dozen more. He was surprised to see how much the Bible had to say on the subject.

It about killed him, he joked, but he did less fishing and Tracy picked someplace they could all go as a family. Ed admits that probably wouldn't have happened if Tracy had not precipitated a small crisis.[7]

That won't work for me. Those are powerful words, and of course, you want to save them for something that matters. How do you know when to hold your ground? When is it worth letting a man grapple with whatever he needs to grapple with?

You don't want to waste that kind of energy on whether or not you eat Mexican food or your distaste for his leather coat—even if he does look like a Mafia hit man. But in every close relationship, there are issues that practically beg you to say no. God may intend to use your "no" in this man's life.

I would suggest that the place to let the crisis happen centers around either one of these two issues:

1. When you believe that the relationship itself will suffer because you are putting up with something that's harmful to you both[8]

2. When you sense that your "no" could open a door in this man's growth that probably won't open if you just continue to go along

I can't emphasize too much how important it is to let go of your anger before you say words like, "That won't work for me." You want this man to wrestle with something that could, eventually, bring some deep changes in his life, remember? So let your words be simple, even respectful—and free of contempt.

Here are some examples of redemptive forms of the kinds of "noes" a woman may have to say to a man she cares about:

- "No, honey, I'm not in favor of spending money we don't have."

- "When you get angry with me and say harsh things, I get the feeling you are really angry with Dad and taking it out on me, your sister. You've got to talk to him. Please stop unloading your anger on me."

- "I know your mother neglected you, but I am not your mother. Just because I can't or don't (whatever) does not mean I'm neglecting you like she did."

In an issue that's been around awhile, you can count on the other party to be surprised. Even shocked. You are not responding the way he expects. You can almost count on him to say some version of, "Change back . . . Respond the way you always do."[9]

This is the crucial part: if you simply keep returning to your position—without getting upset—you will see movement. It may be small, but nine times out of ten, it will be something.

Many a good man would trace the change in his life to a "crisis" with the woman he loves.

DISCOVERING HE HAS WHAT IT TAKES

Buried in the heart of a guy, shielded even from his own eyes, is a longing that's almost an ache. He longs for someone to discover him—to believe, with him and (occasionally) for him, that he has what it takes.[10] In the same way that a man is usually limited in his ability to read the insides of other people, his ability to understand his own masculine soul, with all its capabilities, is a mystery to him as well.

> *Many a good man would trace the change in his life to a "crisis" with the woman he loves.*

That's why he may think he has to save the world . . . when mostly, all that's needed is to show up and do his thing. It's really quite enough.

Paul had a glimpse of this reality in the middle of the mall. He was dodging shoppers with his girlfriend, Shelley, whom he'd been dating for a couple of years. She was telling him about a conversation she'd had with her sister the day before. Once again, she told Paul, she felt about five years old, put down and bested by her older sibling.

Paul was an aspiring college professor, a graduate assistant who taught for a living. He got paid to solve problems of some sort. Shelley's sister was a perennial source of pain in her life.

And Paul couldn't resist the urge to get right in the middle of her feelings and straighten it all out. He would find a solution, or bust.

But this time, for some reason, instead of telling Shelley what to do, he simply said, "Wow, I bet that's hard to live with. I don't know how you put up with that."

Shelley stopped dead in her tracks. That was exactly what she needed to hear. Maybe she wasn't crazy. Her sister *was* a challenge. She told Paul how much his words meant to her.

Paul recounted the experience with me later. "Can you believe that?" he said. "All I did was say, 'I bet that's hard,' and she acted like I'd given her flowers."

I wish I could take a snapshot of a man's face in a moment when he discovers he has what it takes. What is needed from him is often much simpler than he imagines. This thing of fumbling around in a woman's feelings—it's not his strong suit. He feels inadequate to the bone. So it is truly a revelation that his empathy voiced, *because it's a man's voice*, really has an impact. It feels like aloe vera on sunburn—applied by a strong male hand.

Most men don't know how powerful they are. All that bravado is, basically, camouflage and fig leaves. Their lives change, and by that I mean that the deep scared places inside them get less scared, as someone catches them in a glory moment. *What you bring to my life as a man is something I can get nowhere else—and it's good stuff. It's the right stuff.*

A man discovers that his support and words and touch—

his sheer presence—means something. In the words of Elton John's song "Can You Feel the Love Tonight?" perhaps, indeed, there is a king inside.

> *A man changes as he steps into moments of inadequacy . . . and realizes that what he brings to the table is, mysteriously, enough.*

A man changes as he steps into moments of inadequacy, big and small, and realizes that what he brings to the table is, mysteriously, enough.

DO MEN CHANGE?

Let me close where I began. Men do change. Sometimes, they change profoundly. But the process doesn't look like ours. The biggest shifts in their psyches often occur paradoxically, as they face the dragons of defeat. Or those changes happen as the result of being in relationship—most notably his relationship with you.

But the caveat in all this is the remarkable dearth of words announcing the shift in his internal landscape. Sometimes, one sentence from a man is as meaningful as an entire conversation a woman might have with another woman. It's very easy to miss. It's like a town with one traffic light—you can be clear through it before you realize you were there.

In order to become a relational genius with a man, it's

> *In order to become a relational genius with a man, it's crucial to realize how few words may accompany his internal shifts.*

crucial to realize how few words may accompany his internal shifts. It will affect the way you listen to him. Or how you watch for clues in what he does.

It reminds me of a conversation a good friend of mine had with her husband, Jim, as they drifted off to sleep one night. They were mumbling back and forth about something her husband's father said on the phone that day. His dad wanted Jim to sell family stock Jim wasn't ready to sell.

"Why didn't you just tell him no?" my friend said.

"I did," Jim replied, as he began to snore lightly. "But you know, my dad's never had much respect for my opinion."

My friend sat straight up in bed. Jim had never admitted that before: his opinion didn't hold much weight with his father. These are the kinds of moments that are easy to miss. They come out of nowhere and when you least expect them. But they are flashing red lights that a man's perception or his understanding is changing.

Personally, I think a man's mind is roughly analogous to a jukebox in an old country store where some stranger walks up and pushes number thirty-two and the song begins to play. You aren't sure why that song started to play then, but listen up.

You never know how long it will be until number thirty-two plays again.

PART TWO

Loving the Man
You Understand

Chapter 5

EXPECTATIONS

Would you be man enough to be my man?
—"STRONG ENOUGH,"
SHERYL CROW

Keith is a conscientious guy who tries to do the right thing. As an accountant from a large Irish clan in New York, he knows how to work hard. That pays off at the office—he has more tax work than he can handle. Keith's frustration is that all his conscientiousness doesn't seem to count for much at home, with his wife, Polly.

Consider their recent ten-year anniversary. Unfortunately, that event occurred in the middle of tax season. (They married before he became a CPA.) Keith knew ten years was a big deal, so he'd had plans. He made reservations at a restaurant so uptown, Polly had to buy a new dress for the occasion—an inconvenience she rather enjoyed.

The problem is that Polly had plans too. She'd dropped hints for months about how this was the year to go away for a long weekend—someplace romantic, with an ocean or the mountains in view. And no children.

Keith, being the straight-talker he is, would explain to Polly each time she suggested a romantic getaway, "Honey, our anniversary is during tax season. Remember, I can't leave town in tax season."

But Polly had previously been married to an emotionally abusive guy, way too similar to her father, whom she hasn't seen in fifteen years. Anniversaries, gifts, and birthdays were huge things to Polly. She read personal messages in them.

So sure, she knew this was tax season. But she couldn't get past the feeling that if she really mattered to a man, he'd drop everything for her. Why didn't Keith get that, for her, love meant feeling special to a man?

Their anniversary evening was romantic. A table with gorgeous linens, soft music playing, and a view of the city skyline. Polly enjoyed the time, but Keith could tell she was disappointed. At one point, as they were talking about how, in the mercy of God, they'd found each other, Keith said, "You know, honey, I wish you could just *trust* that I love you. I wish it didn't have to be proved."

What Keith also felt was that there had been two men in Polly's past who'd failed her miserably—and he was being sent the bill.

FINDING A TRUE BASELINE

Oh, how easily this kind of thing happens.

Expectations. Freud famously noted that in spite of all his studies, he could never figure out what a woman wanted.

Perhaps the right comeback would be, "What is a woman supposed to want? What, exactly, is she supposed to expect from a man?"

That's a hard question to answer in the current climate. Media and movies portray a guy like he's some big dolt with one thing on his mind, and it's not dinner. You should be grateful if he shaves once a week. He's not like his father—or his grandfather—who by the age of twenty got sent to war, where he learned the rigors of hardship and sacrifice and responsibility, and then came home to a hero's welcome. There is a noticeable lack of shaping male influences these days.

So it's hard to get your bearings about what you should even think about wanting from a guy.[1] Men get mixed messages from us. We might resent a guy's passivity, but we're scared of his power. We worry that he won't do, can't engage, and doesn't commit.

What do right-sized expectations actually look like?

To get at that question, I feel the necessity to anchor this conversation in the larger perspective of how God sees a man. What we look for from the men in our lives won't make much sense unless we start here. So follow me as we look across a huge and fascinating landscape.

In the beginning, God allowed Adam to name each animal in the garden.[2] In ancient understanding, to name something was to take on the responsibility for its protection and care. When God created Eve, it was Adam who gave her the name Woman.[3] God laid a weight of responsibility on the shoulders of a man from the start of things.

So when Eve ate the forbidden fruit, it made total sense why God showed up in Adam's space. "Where are you?" God asked Adam, who was peeking out from behind fig leaves.[4] Adam tried to push the blame back on Eve, inventing the first lame excuse known to man. But God did not let Adam off the hook.

This accountability—God's expectation of a man—continues through the Bible until you come to the most breathtaking requirement of all (something no man can fulfill, really, on his own): "Husbands, love your wives, just as Christ also loved the church and gave Himself up for her."[5]

Think what a call to sacrificial love sounded like when it was first uttered in a culture where women were worth only slightly more than your best cow. *Love your wife as Christ loved the church.* To enter a lifelong, monogamous union between a man and a woman, where a man is required to cherish and provide for his wife, who cannot be divorced on a whim—this was so unusual that it set these Christians apart from the rest of the pagan world. It was a radical departure from the past.

If we take our clues from God about what a man is put on the planet to be and do, then we can only say, with awe, *a lot.* God expects a lot from men.

WHEN ARE YOU EXPECTING TOO MUCH?

Our expectations of a man must be grounded in the way God made him. Understanding creates expectations. And the right kinds of expectations are the golden hinges of relationships. These tell us what to ask for, what to invite—and sometimes, what to insist upon.

So, given that the cultural markers are crazy, and even men aren't sure what it means to be a man these days—then it's no wonder that many

> *Our expectations of a man must be grounded in the way God made him.*

women feel lost. It's easy for us to ricochet between expectations that are too much or way too little. Let's look at both extremes.

The most common place where expectations get inflated are when those expectations are borne of trauma or big disappointments. Like Polly, we can be sending a man the bill for losses we incurred with earlier men in our lives. It happens quite unconsciously. *With this man, I'll finally feel all the love I've missed.*

But no man in the present can make up for a woman's losses in the past. Polly slowly realized that the ache, the empty hole that opened up inside her on special occasions, said more about her than it did about her husband. She was hearing the ghosts of her own insecurities. When she felt her way through her father's abandonment—when she dealt with the baggage of her first marriage—Keith's efforts looked different. She could actually enjoy the evening with him for what it was. She could let herself be loved by this man, in this moment. And Keith didn't have to make up for the past.

Sometimes, loss blows a bunch of smoke in our eyes. And

what gets created in our heads is an idealized man no guy could live up to. Actually, ten men wouldn't be enough.

I think of my friend whose father decided he was gay when she was ten years old. He moved out and lived with his partner. In her dad's place, a larger-than-life man grew in her mind. When she was attracted to a guy and wanted a simple, easy conversation with him, she felt like she was talking to a god. She clammed up and got breathless—and she was sure he didn't like her. She had to face what the loss of her father meant and the conclusions she'd drawn about men—so she could actually relate to a regular guy and enjoy him.

My own version of great expectations is what I call "the composite man." I don't realize what I'm assembling in my head until I catch myself cutting and pasting . . . men. This composite guy has the stunning intelligence of Dick and the energy of Sam and the business ability of Harry. And oh, I especially like the way Steve always refills the water glasses and coffee cups when we eat at their place. Who can live up to that combination? I am creating the myth of the total package—which is ironic, since I know I'm not one myself.

You could say it's a woman's version of polygamy.

The plain truth about men is that, like us, they only glow

> *Each man has his own mix of strengths and weaknesses. And often, you don't get a particular strength unless you accept its corresponding weakness.*

in the dark for a while. Each man has his own mix of strengths and weaknesses. And often, you don't get a particular strength unless you accept its corresponding weakness. This intelligent, absent-minded guy who can invent computer software in his head may never pack the car well. Or remember your birthday without a flag that appears on his BlackBerry.

Or think how much you loved the laid-back, easygoing guy you married. That same trait may mean that the deep, philosophical conversations you crave will be with other people, not him. As my aunt Maude used to say, mountain woman that she was, "You can't teach a chicken to swim."

Sometimes I have to remind myself of stuff like this. Or I will miss my life. I will fail to enjoy and appreciate the man in front of my eyes—as he is. Which, after all, is a pretty good package when you get right down to it.

EXPECTATIONS THAT ARE TOO SMALL

There is, of course, another end of the expectation spectrum. It's the malady of expecting too little from a man—and frankly, it's more common in these emancipated days than it used to be. This is a case in point.

Janet was particularly attracted to men who needed her. She lived in the hope that, someday, a guy would appreciate the great things she added to his life.

One fine October day, when the leaves were just past their peak, she struck up a conversation at her nephew's soccer match with an athletic guy named Kyle. Before long, they became a twosome. A few months turned into a few years, and Janet began to question where their relationship was headed.

Finally, she said, "You know, being in limbo—neither single nor married—is really hard for me."

Kyle got the picture. After Janet helped him pick out an engagement ring, they set a wedding date. Once they were married, she kept their lives perking along like a smooth, oiled machine.

Nothing about this arrangement seemed terribly abnormal to Janet. Sure, she wished that Kyle took more initiative in about any category you could name. But she enjoyed his sense of humor. And they had such great memories together— kayaking mountain streams, spending countless nights under a sea of stars. She really loved this guy.

Janet did not realize something was missing. By the time she was twelve and noticing the world, a prescription drug habit had deeply eroded her father's life. His professional world disappeared and what she remembers is more phantom than father—a shadow of the man he once was. Her mother became, understandably, everyone's long-suffering pillar of strength.

"Normal" for Janet was a man who leaned on a woman. She got her doctorate in biology, and when Kyle's teaching job stagnated, she was the one who researched other job possibilities. She buffered his testy moments with friends and made sure he called his parents. Occasionally, Kyle would make odd comments that Janet remembered later, like omens she had missed.

"I don't feel like a man with you," he'd say—or something close to that. Janet kept hoping Kyle would take hold of life and find some confidence. But more and more, he just seemed to resent hers.

Still, she was caught by surprise when he had an affair.

It seems like the worst kind of bee sting when you are penalized for bringing so much to a relationship with a man. Everything in us shouts, "That's not fair!" And really, it isn't fair.

Our culture rewards the woman who is competent. She walks away with big prizes. Doors for success open wide to her talents. In personal relationships with men, though, all that ability can bite if it blinds you to the strength a man is uniquely meant to supply. You won't be looking for it—or noting its absence.

Expecting too little from a man may mean, unfortunately, that too little is what you get. That's why our conversation has to begin with God—and not with our fathers or any of the men we may currently know. What a man has to offer is what God has put in him—even if he hasn't realized it yet. It's still there. And it's right for you to want his strength and his perspective and his support in the ways men give that.

Without this understanding—this expectation—then we become, inevitably, some distortion of the vigor we long for.

> *Expecting too little from a man may mean, unfortunately, that too little is what you get.*

Or like Janet, we can easily attach ourselves to a man who elevates passivity to an art form.

Of the two extremes, having expectations that are too little may well be more dangerous.

WHAT TO LOOK FOR

So this man won't be the superman who can deliver you from all your fears. He's not your savior. He can't love you with a love that never fails. He is only a man.

And yet, there is something wonderful here—something quite different from you. He is a tonic you really need.

Having right-sized expectations of a guy hinges on your willingness to hope that he will show up. His perspective can open up doors in your head you hadn't thought to knock on. His support gives you permission to believe that what God says about you is really true. His strong back braves the wind coming at you. And you'll get this glimpse . . . of him.

Such a hope is rooted in a deepening understanding of what God puts men on the planet for, and why he brings some important ones into your life. It takes literal shape in moments—in glimpses—as you become aware of being a woman. It's as though something "other" brushes past you for a second. Sometimes, this *otherness* practically envelops you. It takes your breath away. But if you aren't aware, if you don't even acknowledge what you long for—you can miss it entirely.

You can be standing knee-deep in a river of water and dying of thirst.

Let me offer you a true story that illustrates some small piece of what it means to let yourself receive a man.

Wanda always wondered if there was a man out there who could handle her size. She was the daughter of a basketball coach, an Amazon woman with a six-foot-eleven frame and more pounds than she wanted packed inside.

Wanda's personality was as big as her person. It was as if she filled up a room with conversation and laughter. Wanda never met a stranger, and she dated a lot of men. She was every guy's best girl friend, but she was not the woman they fell in love with.

Part of the problem could be traced to one soul-rattling moment when she was at her heaviest—at the tender age of fifteen. Her father was known around town for his coaching, but only his children knew what he was like when he drank. One evening he was taking Wanda to watch a rival team's game. He'd had a few too many when Wanda came down the stairs.

Her father took one look at her and said, "I'm not taking you to a basketball game. I'm ashamed to be seen with you."

It's tragic the way words can be said under the influence that would never be spoken dead sober. For Wanda, no apology could undo the damage. The last thing she wanted was to be some man's embarrassment.

So from that point in her life, when she was hanging out with a guy, she made sure she walked five paces ahead. *Give him a little breathing room—he won't want anyone to think we're together.* It wasn't the easiest way to carry on a conversation, but Wanda managed.

The summer she turned thirty, she met Joe at a youth camp where they were both counselors between regular teaching jobs. He was five years younger, but just as tall. By the end of June, he was finding excuses to help her with her campers. Finally, he asked her out to dinner.

Wanda did her usual thing. She got out of the car and started walking fast. But this man ran to catch up with her. Joe put his hand on the small of her back and walked alongside. Wanda says that this small gesture changed her life. It was the first time she had felt attractive to a man—and worth something. He wasn't ashamed of her.

Three children and twenty years later, she can still feel the significance of his touch.

To live with right-sized expectations of men is to stay alert on the inside, aware of what you need, and open to what God brings into your life through a man.

> *To live with right-sized expectations of men is to stay alert on the inside, aware of what you need, and open to what God brings into your life through a man.*

When he is sweating bullets over qualifying for a loan to buy your first home, you're being cared for by him. If it's his hand stroking your arm in the middle of the night, you can go back to sleep. When he says, "Honey, it will be okay. I'll take care of it," something relaxes inside you. God means for you to enjoy that.

It's right to want a strength you can lean on.

It's right for you to expect something from a man.

EXPECTATIONS AND YOUR OWN HEART

When I encourage you to keep your heart open, I realize I'm inviting you to a harder way to live.

There's an old story that gets repeated, over and over. We want something from each other that we can't get. We hope . . . we expect . . . and if we get disappointed enough, we may fold our hearts into little triangles like a flag we store in the bottom dresser drawer. And we get on with life.

But something beautiful is lost there inside us, and between us.

I am inviting you to a more costly, vulnerable path in your relationships with men. If you let yourself hope, expect, and want what a man is capable of giving—the best of what God has put in him—then there will be stinging disappointments along the way. When all is said and done, each of us is just one sinner trying imperfectly to love another sinner—and there are times we miss the other person by a country mile.

But the vulnerability and the hope is a form of trusting God. For any man and woman who claim Christ, there really is a Third Party present.[6] When I'm disappointed by a man, there is Someone to whom I can turn—and he never turns me away. This is reality—as real as the chair I sit on while I write these words.

I know that when you screw up your nerve and ask a man for something you need, and he gets intimidated or switches the subject, it's a miserable experience. Visions of curling up in a fetal position may flash before your eyes. But it's not the disappointment that actually undoes you. You'll get over feeling disappointed.

No, the toxic part is this: drawing the erroneous conclusion that you're an awful woman or a weak one to want something from a man in the first place. *Buck up, honey.* That's the internal dialogue that undoes a woman.

You are meant to want something from a man.

I'm inviting you to the harder path of hope and expectation because it leads—eventually—to something much richer in your relationships. It can free up the bondage inside your own heart. Your relationship with a man will slowly get deeper and more real. And most important, God will become to you, in actuality, the father, husband, brother, and friend you've always hoped for. You may, in retrospect, see a bit of disappointment as your ticket to winning the lottery.

> *I'm inviting you to the harder path of hope and expectation because it leads—eventually—to something much richer in your relationships.*

Jesus said, simply and straightforwardly, "Enter through the narrow gate; for the gate is wide and the way is broad that leads to destruction, and there are many who enter through it. For the gate is small and the way is narrow that leads to life, and there are few who find it."[7]

This principle holds true in relationships too. What looks and feels easy doesn't take you very far. The path of hope and expectation in your relationships with men is harder. It triggers more vulnerability on your part. It's a wilder ride. But this hope is rooted in the truth of how God has made you—and what he means for a man to be.

God honors a pattern of vulnerability that's grounded in truth and hope. It is, after all, the way his Son lived.

Chapter 6

RESPECT

All I'm asking, is for a little respect when you come home,
—"RESPECT"
ARETHA FRANKLIN

We have dear Aretha Franklin to thank for making the word famous. Gang members commit acts of violence as a bizarre means of earning this intangible affirmation. Average men speak the word in reverential tones. Even the apostle Paul highlighted its importance. You could say it's the holy grail men search for all their lives.

I am, of course, talking about respect.

Now, I confess that I have always found it difficult to wrap my head around notions of respect—and how it could mean so much to a man. If you want to discuss a woman's longing for love and security, I totally resonate. That makes such logical, emotional sense. Life, after all, is uncertain. Houses burn down, relationships are forever in flux, and we may never be able to retire. But respect? How can that be so necessary in the scheme of things?

Add to this confusion the fact that women can carry

around some wild misconceptions of what it means to offer a man respect. *"Oh, you're right, you're right," she tells him, as she falls at his feet. But, really . . . she thinks he's crazy.* Lots of women equate respect with a string of adulations, while both parties ignore a problem the size of an elephant.

The true nature of respect, though, is a far cry from tiptoeing around the fragile ego of a man who just can't handle you—or the tough pieces of his own life. And that is what I'd like to explore in these pages.

WHAT RESPECT FEELS LIKE

Fundamentally, respect is about seeing a man. It means believing he has something unique and valuable to offer. He has stuff that's slightly different from your stuff and is, therefore, stuff you need. Male stuff. And by that, I don't just mean rewarding anatomical features. I mean there's an actual man in there, capable of leading and giving and showing up in difficult moments. Even though he might have disappointed you a hundred times.

What does respect feel like to a man, though? And why is it something that feels essential to his being? I've shopped that question around with many men through the years. The form of respect a man usually mentions first—indeed, the most obvious form of respect—is his longing for a woman who knows him and loves him to be his foremost cheerleader.

Or as a man who'd recently started his own company

> *The form of respect*
> *a man usually*
> *mentions first . . .*
> *is his longing*
> *for a woman who*
> *knows him and*
> *loves him to be his*
> *foremost cheerleader.*

said, "It's my wife's vote of confidence that makes me want to bust my tail."

It's kind of like a man sees himself out there on the field of life. Maybe it's a cold November day with the threat of snow in the air. Ten people are coming at him with black smudges under their eyes, and they'd like to knock him into nowhere. But if he can see your face lining the field—if, somehow, you still believe in him in spite of everything—then maybe he stands a decent chance of moving the ball closer to the goal.

So whether you're talking about a son or husband or brother or just a good friend, this man wants to feel that you are truly in his corner. You may know where his birthmark is, how bad he hates broccoli, his struggle with speaking in public. Paradoxically, it is because you know his weaknesses that he needs to feel, all the more, that you believe in him. He needs to hear, with some regularity, what you see in him that's good and right and true.

The irony, of course, is that in a close relationship, a strange kind of atrophy is at work. You're probably the person most aware of his flaws. It's much too easy to fixate on a man's weaknesses. After all, aren't his strengths obvious? Aren't they what attracted you to him in the first place?

If our focus becomes shoring up a man's weaknesses, we may grow blind to what he does so well. When we lose sight of his strengths, our voices sound more like black crows carping in his ear. Forget the cheerleader biz.

So whether the man in front of you is your son or son-in-law, a friend, a man you work with, or your husband—you want to be intentional with what you say. As the embroidered tapestry above my friend's desk says, "Words are so powerful they should only be used to heal, to bless, and to prosper."

It's not disingenuous (in fact, it's downright smart) to put words to the strength you see in a man. He will never outgrow his need to hear it. *Never.* Even if we are choking on the effects of a mistake he's made, we must try (hard) to not lose sight of the man himself, or his strengths.

Having your support and advocacy is what a man feels most acutely as respect. In a marriage there is an additional saving grace. Sex is a regular, two-for-one special. Through the magic of touch, sex translates directly into respect, by-passing the need for words. It's a direct pipeline to a man's inner being.

Sex is a wordless cheer, you might say.

Perhaps the closest we ever come to understanding what respect means to a man, though, is this: for a man, respect is the rough equivalent of your own best moments of feeling truly loved.

A MAN FEELS RESPECT FROM
A WOMAN WHEN SHE . . .

- solicits his opinion or perspective as though he might have something truly unique to offer;

- expresses her confidence in him by asking him to do the hard thing that is also the right thing;

- sleeps with her husband . . . euphemistically speaking;

- refuses to attack his character, even when he's failed her or others;

- realizes her vulnerabilities and values his protection;

- can name her own mistakes and her need of him;

- allows him (on occasion) to offer a solution to a problem she considers vexing, thereby exploring some possibilities she might not have otherwise;

- believes he can come back from failure or defeat.

NEEDING THIS MAN

You have probably figured out that respect is not always about sweet, cheerful moments between a man and a woman. Though, as I say, most relationships could use more of those.

I want to explore respect in its less common forms. There are facets of respect just as crucial as being a man's cheerleader—and they're no less important because they are less obvious. Let me see if I can illustrate what I mean.

Suzanne's jeans didn't fit the way they used to, and the wrinkles around her eyes bore uncanny resemblance to her mother's. Some days she felt like a hamster on a treadmill, waving at people as she went around and around. She wanted to slow down. She especially wanted to reconnect with her husband, Joe.

She missed the way they used to grab a quiet evening out someplace, with their cell phones turned off. A few hours, the tiniest drop of romance. The way Joe would take her hand and say, "We're going out." He'd pick a movie or a new restaurant—and the demands of life would evaporate for a while. And Suzanne would feel he was actually thinking about the two of them.

But Joe owned a landscape business with stiff competitors, and their children were nearing the age for college. By the time he got home, he was spent. They used to talk at night and share their day. Now they did their own thing . . . and then fell in bed exhausted.

Suzanne could sense that they were drifting apart. She felt

lonely a lot. "Honey," she told him, "I really need for the two of us to do more together—just us. I've missed that. Actually, I've missed you."

"What do mean you've missed me?" Joe responded. "It's not like I've gone anywhere."

Suzanne explained that, really, he had gone somewhere. Maybe they both had. "We used to enjoy just going out, sitting in a coffee shop, catching a movie. You're the guy who would listen to me think out loud. We had a good time."

Joe reminded her that sometimes their good time was spoiled by a bad mood or a discussion that got too heated.

"I know, I know," she admitted, "but that doesn't change the fact that you are the man I want to be with. And these days, it seems like the best of you is being given to other people, out there in the big world. Like I said, I miss you."

Suzanne needs this man. Perhaps this sounds too simple, but needing a man is one of the most crucial aspects of respect. It's a facet we easily skip past. If you've been in a close relationship long enough to be disappointed by a man, you know how logical it seems to stop wanting him.

Have you considered, though, that to actually let yourself need a man—his perspective or his presence or his support—is at the heart of offering him respect? You are saying that what he brings to your life can't be replaced by someone else, even your best girlfriend.

I read recently about a woman whose husband spent two tours in Iraq as a sniper. When he came home, his nerves were shot. The least little thing made him anxious and irritable. As he recuperated, his wife said that she got more and more glimpses of his old self—his better self, the man she remembered. "Where have *you* been?" she'd say to him. "Bring the man I knew home to me."

A form of that happens in every close relationship with a man. You get glimpses of something wonderful in him. It feels like sitting for a few moments in the shade of an oak tree

> *Letting yourself need a man, even when he's failed you, is utterly foundational to offering him respect.*

while you exhale and catch your breath. But life piles on, and sometimes the best gets hidden. Your need of this man, in his better state, is a vote of confidence that he exists. It's an invitation for that man to come out from under the pile and join you.

Letting yourself need a man, even when he's failed you, is utterly foundational to offering him respect.

THE ETERNAL CYCLE

There's a script men and women play out with each other— and this script causes notions of need and respect to get tangled up. It's a cycle that goes something like this: you want something from this man, but he doesn't interpret your need as a compliment or a vote of confidence. It does not make his day. Rather, your desire or need hits the trip wire of his sense of inadequacy.

Men and women dance this dance ad infinitum.

See if this feels familiar. Every woman has her moments, right? And while you try to not be crazy on the same day, if something is bothering you—if, for a hundred reasons, you just aren't in a good place—then you might need to talk your way through it. Maybe you need for a man to sit in a chair and listen, even though he could recite it all by heart. Yes, you have girlfriends you could call. But girlfriends aren't a husband— and they aren't a man.

As you might have experienced, though, listening to an upset woman isn't on the list of big thrills for most guys. Sometimes, you have to wade through his impatience and his own need to fix something he can't fix. He might switch the subject or quietly exit the room—and you could feel like you're standing naked on the street corner.

All kinds of things can happen when your need taps into his fear of his own inadequacy. But that's no good reason to run for cover or bury your heart.

For sure, you have to wade through your own fear that he'll get so perturbed he'll pull away and leave you high and dry.

All kinds of things can happen when your need taps into his fear of his own inadequacy. But that's no good reason to run for cover or bury your heart. I'm not suggesting you wig out on him, but if you hang in there—and hanging in there is a form of respect—you will both slowly get somewhere.

In this perennial dance, it helps if you're clear about

things. Tell him something like, "Just let me work my way through this, please. You don't have to fix it. I need for you to listen and hear me out. Right now, it's not advice or a prescription that will help me." Or maybe, you really do need his insight. So ask him, how does he see this?

Slowly, a man's fears will shrink to a more manageable size—as will yours. It's not easy for a man to be with a woman who, in the moment, is not a happy camper and he can't remedy the problem. But, oh, the grace of a man's presence when it feels like life is caving in on you and he can just hear you out. Listening is love in its purest form.

There are plenty of times, though, when you may literally ache for a response that's actually somewhere inside him— and he can't put it in words. Simple things, really—like a moment when you just need for a man to say, "I understand." Or "I bet that really hurts." Some women would say they just want a man to hold them. Some simple thing . . . and it would make all the difference in the world.

When you don't get the response you long for, it's tempting to roll up the welcome mat of your heart. After all, Christ is present in ways that, while they aren't tangible, are more real than any human being. Sometimes, he is the only one you can turn to. When you need a man's comfort or reassurance or understanding—and he can't go there—it's a tremendous gift that God knows you intimately. He "gets you." It's almost better than a person, because God never withholds his love. He never runs away.

But, except in the rarest situations, that is not meant to

> *There is something redemptive about the messy process of needing someone with skin on and having to work through your own fears and disappointments as you go along.*

be an exclusive experience between you and God. There is something redemptive about the messy process of needing someone with skin on and having to work through your own fears and disappointments as you go along. God is present then as well.

The humility of telling a man what you need him to say can be strangely medicinal. It's a bit like holding up cue cards. "What I need to hear is that I have your support even if this other situation falls apart." Or something like that. It helps to give a man a verbal clue, to "hold up a cue card" of what you actually need to hear in a stressful moment.

I am the first to admit that it's wonderful when a man intuitively knows what you need to hear. But lots of men flounder to find the words a woman is searching for—words they'd like to offer if they knew what on earth they were! So if you find yourself, on occasion, having to hold up some cue cards, take heart. It's surprisingly validating. And it sure beats feeling resentful because a man doesn't say or do what seems obvious to you as a woman.

Even when a man doesn't quite get it right, the pleasure of letting yourself need a man is a wonderful thing. And needing him is some of the best respect you can offer.

MORE ACTION, LESS TALK

There is another form of respect that doesn't depend so much on words. It's more about taking a particular sort of action—more "do" than "say."

If you live around a man for any length of time, you will know what he's avoiding. You may sense what he's afraid of even more than he does. And if you're the kind of woman who's intuitive and good at meeting needs, you may fill in the broken places for a man without a moment's hesitation. You can be the glue in all his important relationships. Actually, a woman can become a man's own personal bottle of Alka-Seltzer.

That may not be the most respectful thing you could do for him.

If there's a transcendent nature to relationships, if we are created in the image of God with a gender that has meaning, then you could "fill in" for him until the cows come home and you will not be able to duplicate what a man brings to the picture. Your touch won't feel like his. Your voice won't sound the same. It will not be enough. Nor will he supply what you supply.

So, sometimes, respect means letting the empty place scream its own scream.

I think of my friend whose distraught daughter called long-distance to talk with her dad. When she answered the phone, her husband edged out of the room, mouthing, "*You talk to her*," because he hates conflict. My friend is good at smoothing over sticky situations. But she's wise enough to know her limits. So respectfully speaking, my friend quietly handed her husband the phone. Their daughter had called to talk to her father. And the two of them would have to work it out.

> *We aren't called
> to be each other's
> chief enabler.
> We are called
> to live for
> the true work of love
> and transformation
> in us both.*

Joe came into marriage with Suzanne having some difficult history with his widowed mother. He'd really prefer to not see her. He could go for months and not contact her. He and Suzanne talked—and they talked. "You can't ignore your mother," Suzanne would say. And Joe would reply, "But she makes me feel like I'm ten years old." And another three months would go by.

Finally, Suzanne invited his mother to visit for the weekend.

"You did what?" Joe said. "You invited my mother to stay here?"

He was shocked, but he knew Suzanne was right. Suzanne stopped talking and *did something*—out of the wild hope and fundamental respect that Joe was man enough to find his way through the impasse.

Suzanne admits it was a hard weekend. She could feel all Joe's anxiety—he was like a chicken on a hot rock. But that weekend broke the ice. It was a small, important step for Joe in learning how to handle an insecure mother who didn't have the power to shrink him into a ten-year-old—unless he let her.

What I'm really saying is that if you believe God is at work in someone, you want to resist the urge to buffer a broken place in him when pain is actually needed for any true hope of change or healing. It's hard to let the discomfort be there. It's even harder if, for some reason, it's thrown back at you as though you're the problem. But, honestly, we aren't called to be each other's chief enabler. We are called to live for the true work of love and transformation in us both.

Respect, genuine respect, can bring some uncomfortable moments when you both may actually feel worse before you feel better.

SHARING YOUR HEART

Let me mention one other facet of showing a man respect that we don't commonly consider. There is a dignity—a sense of walking upright—that God embeds in a man's being. You want to honor that dignity, which means that you count his weight or significance in your life. It's embodied in the things you love most about him. And it's also mirrored in those times when you are so disappointed you could cry a bucket of tears.

Grief, then, has its place in a relationship—and it can play a crucial role in respecting a man. Lots of women (and I'm one of them) feel anger long before they figure out what has made them sad. But grief is a reflection of genuine hopes dashed. And disappointed hope is rooted in respect. Let me offer an example.

Suzanne has other men in her life. Her brother-in-law, Jake, graduated from an ROTC program near the top of his class. Jake was the kind of good-looking, accomplished guy a woman spots across a crowded room, and Suzanne was thrilled when he fell in love with her younger sister, Margaret. They had a storybook romance. Since Margaret was so young when their mother died, it seemed a fitting grace.

Jake left this storybook picture, though, so he could lead a platoon of men in Afghanistan. The pressures of war in a mountainous desert and losing men he cared about took a toll. He accepted the overtures of another woman who was also feeling lonely and away from home. Jake was miserable with guilt. So he came clean with Margaret, who was devastated. And Suzanne was there to pick up the pieces, to bear the full force of the pain, until Jake returned.

What was Suzanne supposed to do when Jake came home? She had felt all Margaret's pain—and her own as well. This was the brother-in-law she welcomed into the family, a man she celebrated, a guy she thought wasn't capable of screwing up this badly.

It would be so tempting to just swallow the elephant, let time go by, and pretend the affair never happened. The family would gather again with lots of uneasy small talk . . . and nobody would look Jake in the eyes.

But Suzanne couldn't live a lie that easily. So she waited for the right moment, and then she said quietly to Jake, "We've got to talk about this—you and me. I'm the one who's been here with my sister as she's cried herself to sleep."

Jake had been dreading this moment. Yet in an odd way, he also seemed relieved. It was easier to face the truth than to bury it.

Suzanne began by admitting that she could wring his neck. She talked about how disappointed she was by him, how much better she thought he was than this. She shared what it was like to try to comfort Margaret until he came home. She shared her grief—a hope deferred that had made her heart sick.[1]

Sharing her grief, speaking the truth, made it possible for Suzanne to forgive and to look this man in the eye again. Her vulnerability qualified as respect because it affirmed an essential aspect of Jake as a man. He wasn't a reed blowing in the wind; he was a man whose actions had an impact. His choices mattered; their consequences were felt by others. Real men face that head-on. And the grief and tears of some very real woman may be just the thing God uses to call him back to the man he wants to be.

In most any close relationship, grief trumps anger—even though anger may be the first thing you feel. It's not easy to get that vulnerable with any man. But to feel the lack of a man's support is to say there is support he could give. Or to note his absence means his presence really matters to you. So grief can be a truly legitimate form of respect.

AN ACT OF FAITH

Offering respect to a man is a small act of faith. You see something real and true in him, knowing he's a work in process. If a man always has to wait to merit your respect, he will feel like a Boy Scout trying to earn a badge.

> *Offering respect to a man invites him to look up, in search of the God who made him, as he reaches inside for what God has put in him.*

Offering respect to a man invites him to look up, in search of the God who made him, as he reaches inside for what God has put in him. Respect is the oxygen in the air he breathes. It's what makes him feel like a man.

Here is an interesting two-week experiment someone once challenged me to try: see how many moments you can nab where you intentionally put into words something you value or respect about this man who matters to you. The experiment was harder than I thought. I didn't realize how much I take a man's strengths for granted—or how quick I was to comment on what needed improvement.

The real eye-opener is the look that quickly passes over a man's face when he even hears the word *respect*.

Verbalizing what you appreciate makes you even more sensitive to respect in its more subtle forms. Like realizing your need for him. Or being willing to ask for the support he can uniquely offer. Or sharing your grief when it's really the backside of believing better of him.

It's a relief to realize that you don't have to completely agree with a man to respect him. You don't have to tiptoe around his ego or be his emotional glue. Just put a few words to what you genuinely admire. His longing for respect is like our longing for security and love.

It's not going away anytime this side of heaven.

Chapter 7

CONFLICT

Sometimes I wonder if men and women really suit each other.
Perhaps they should live next door and just visit now and then.
—KATHARINE HEPBURN

There is a sneaky little requirement, hidden in the fine print of your quest to have geniuslike relationships with men—especially the man you love. You've got to be able to wade through a bit of disagreement. Maybe even a lot of disagreement.

Personally, I hate conflict in a relationship. I prefer to tip-toe around difficult topics or call a truce before the issues get well aired. Why spoil a lovely evening? Why suffer through misunderstanding and hurt feelings? Harmony is so much easier. If the good times with a man are like a three-course meal with tiramisu for dessert, then why eat black-eyed peas with turnip greens?

I admit this reluctantly, but I know it's true: there's really something to be had from those black-eyed peas.

Of course, most conflict with a man who matters to you isn't planned for. *Okay . . . Thursday morning, when I've had enough sleep and I'm thinking rationally, we can talk about why I cringe when your mother's car pulls in the driveway.* No, there's rarely a plan in place. It's more like one of you stepped on a land mine you forgot was there and *boom!* Harsh words are said. Looks are given. And old history gets repeated . . . again.

You may have heard the classic advice given to a man and a woman considering marriage. Perhaps someone even said these words to you: "Make sure you've had a few good fights before you marry this guy." It's a gentle way of saying that you won't live in the same space long without clashing together like two pool balls. Can you clash and come out alive? Now, that's the question.

Yet there's much to be gained from conflict in a close relationship, especially if you think of disagreement as an extended dialogue. After all, big things in your heart are at stake. So the truly crucial conversations can only happen in small increments over a long time, as you both can bear it. It's a complicated thing to put a man and a woman in the same bed and the same emotional space—for, say, longer than a month. Thus it's quite possible that understanding where you're each coming from—and what changes need to be made—may qualify as a lifelong dialogue, indeed.

> *There's much to be gained from conflict in a close relationship, especially if you think of disagreement as an extended dialogue.*

In this process, I want to employ a familiar image, a helpful metaphor I keep in mind myself. Most of us have one of these in our homes. It's the proverbial walk-in closet. You live in the rest of your house. Happy things happen around a kitchen table. Lifelong memories are made in the family room. Warm and sexual things take place in a bedroom. But in your walk-in closet, you store some necessary items. They sit there, waiting for you. They aren't going anywhere soon. At some crucial time, you'll need that stuff.

The kind of conflict that's actually an extended dialogue can be like that. In fact, it needs to be like that. To live well with a man, you must be able to take an issue off the shelf and sort through it, a piece at a time. Then when you've gone as far as you can in a particular disagreement, the issue goes back in the walk-in closet of your relationship—and you get on with your life together. You laugh around the kitchen table and you enjoy sex. Until the next time it comes up.

> *Any lasting relationship with a man . . . can only be forged out of two decent forgivers.*

I'm not implying this process is neat and tidy. Sometimes, two perfectly sane adults discuss something bothering one of them with the cool logic of trained negotiators. And other times, this ongoing "dialogue" hits you on a bad hair day and erupts in a flat-out argument. It can happen to the best of people.

So part of the skill you're developing is the ability to repair from hurt—either the pain you feel or the pain you cause. Any lasting relationship with a man, be it a son or brother or husband or good friend, can only be forged out of two decent forgivers.

PEEKING INSIDE THE BOX

I want to invite you into the lives of two friends, whose particulars have been changed to protect their identities. But their conflict is a common one. One only need switch the faces around.

Dan owns a reliable pharmacy in a busy part of town. He's a reserved, efficient guy, which makes him good at what he does. Even though he just turned forty, older folks still think of him as "Frank's boy"—Frank being the gregarious, wildly successful entrepreneur who built the first big mall around. Dan may never come close to filling his father's shoes. His example, though, explains why Dan counts pills all day and then works into the wee hours on a plan to buy another pharmacy.

Dan is actually quite attached to his wife, Laura, though she disputes that claim.

His best friend in college introduced them. Dan privately feels it was the coup of the century that he married her, since Laura had recently broken up with a guy she was crazy about. Somewhere in Dan's head he still wonders if he was the man she chose—or the man she settled for. He's never been entirely sure.

Their problem is that Dan's ideas of "togetherness" are

much different than Laura's. He feels like he's been with Laura when they're under the same roof—or sharing the same bed. His cup of intimacy is filled rather easily. A little sex, a bit of conversation, and Dan is good to go. He's back to acquiring pharmacies and counting pills. If he wants to seriously unwind, it's at the end of a fishing pole or a golf club. And he'd love for Laura to join him, but that's not even on her radar screen.

So as you can guess, they argue over little things, which are really just camouflage for the main thing. *Do you want to be with me? Do I matter to you? Why are you always going out the door and I'm here, feeling like I have to handle everything myself?*

Historically, when Dan and Laura tangle over this, it's a bad scene. All the hurt Laura has stored up comes out in a torrent of angry words. (She could have been a trial lawyer, Dan believes.) "Look, my mother spent years in bed with multiple sclerosis, and she died when I was in college. I've had enough of feeling alone!" she says.

Dan's at a loss for the right words to say. Sometimes, he just sits like a totem pole and mentally reviews his golf swing, trying to calm down. *Why, exactly, does she think I'm counting pills or working a deal to buy another pharmacy? Why do I get up in the morning, if not to create something for her and the kids?*

Occasionally, though, Laura will trip Dan's switch and he blows. "I can spend the whole weekend with you, and it's never enough. Never enough! I can't hold your hand all day.

One of us has to get out there and get it done. You take my hard work for granted."

WHY WE NEED A STRATEGY FOR CONTAINMENT

Like I say, the real conflict in a close relationship has to be understood as an extended dialogue—small bits unraveled over years. My hope is to help you live long enough to tell the tale.

In any conflict, there's the part that's obvious and the part that's hidden. That's why it takes so long to understand yourself or the other person. What can't be said often enough is that, when the two of you are going at it, there are four people in the room: two adults and two kids. If there were only adults present in Dan and Laura's story, things would get simple fast. This is not rocket science. One person needs more time together than the other person, not unlike when one person needs more sex than the other does.

> *In any conflict, there's the part that's obvious and the part that's hidden.*

So if conflict were only about devising solutions, Dan and Laura would have a date night at least twice a month. They'd talk, just the two of them, before Dan started studying business acquisitions at night. They'd probably have a little more sex because, sometimes, one thing kind of leads to another. And then Laura wouldn't secretly believe that was the *only* kind of togetherness that really interested Dan.

But in any conflict that persists, there are also two kids wreaking havoc who are, in their own way, scared spitless. They've got their fears and they've got their tears—and no one's ever heard them out. An intimate relationship, like marriage, is a second chance. It's as close as we'll ever get to rewriting our inner story.

It's why we keep restaging the conflict.

I want to explain why this process is the mercy of God in our lives. In any of us in whom the honor of his name rests because he has made us his through Christ, there's a deep excavation happening. As unbelievable as it seems some days, his image is being shaped into the mud of our souls. That's where our fears are dug in deep. And we work hard to keep everyone, especially ourselves, fooled into thinking we're okay. God isn't fooled.

He has our number. God comes after us—after this mud at the bottom of our scared and sinful souls. He comes after us in various ways, but he's always present in the form of someone we love. Someone we want to love us. Only when there are huge heart matters at stake will we let his light into our own particular darkness. Only then.

That's the spiritual basis for the strenuous task of containing a conflict so that it can become the deep spade work of God in your own soul. Unraveling conflict will help you face your fears. It exposes the lies we hide behind. Sometimes, it even forces us to admit how distorted our image of God actually is.

In this way, and often unknowingly, we are used by God in each other's life to air out the scared places in our hearts we never knew were there—until they hurt.

HOW CONTAINMENT HAPPENS

So the black-eyed peas of a relationship are quite important. And you really must have a walk-in closet where you can store this conflict when you need to, because, as you know, the conflict cannot be allowed to take over your life.

Practically speaking, the goal is to be able to talk about an important matter a little longer . . . a little deeper . . . over the course of time, without one or the other of you freaking out. Here's what constitutes this highly scientific term, *freaking out*:

- Verbally hacking into the other person—either in tone of voice, volume, or content of words[1]

- Shutting down, commonly known as *stonewalling*, which is just like it sounds: "becoming a stone wall"

Men and women have their own specialty areas of freaking out. Let's deal with a man's first. Again, his reaction reflects his brain structure. Since his amygdala is larger and testosterone pumps through his veins, he has a quicker flight-or-fight response. His blood pressure and heart rate rise faster than yours, and they stay elevated longer.

It's not kosher for a guy to ram his fist through the wall. So in an effort to calm down, the vast majority of men (when they feel threatened) will stonewall a woman if things get too intense. Like Dan, he turns into an expressionless totem pole. He may literally back out of the room. It can be incredibly frustrating to be on the receiving end—it's like he's been spirited away by aliens and has left you in the dust.

You may think that behind this expressionless face, nothing's happening. It's amazing to discover that, in fact, his internal indicators are off the charts. (Oh, what a glorious day, when men could finally be wired to computers that record their inner workings.) Behind the stonewall, he's been emotionally hijacked, sometimes called "flooding." The buzzers in him are going off so loudly that he can't sort through the particulars. He's overwhelmed.

It's the oddest thing to watch, because a guy appears to be distracted, maybe even bored.

This woman who's upset with him is asking for something he's not sure he has. Sometimes even the simplest things can be heard as criticism. The whole picture can turn you into a crazy woman. Here's this big, lanky guy with more muscles in his arm than you have in your whole body, and he's "freaking out" inside because you're upset with him?

Apparently, we burrow our way into man's psyche more than we think. Our voices matter (sometimes too much). Listen to this expert on men as he describes the way a man feels:

Women will never be able to understand men until they realize that the most frightening thing in life for men is the anger of women. . . . A woman's anger is as terrifying to a man as the wrath of an angry god. We don't hear what a woman says when she's angry and we strap ourselves in, turn off the receiver and wait in terror for the storm to pass.[2]

Now it is true that these gender scripts during conflict can get reversed. There are plenty of angry, verbal men out there—and good women have been known to stonewall (though, usually, it's when they feel too hurt to speak). But this is not the norm.

The more common form of "freaking out" for a woman is some form of a verbal jab. And this makes sense. What we lack in physical size must be compensated for with something equally powerful, like words. Women learn that early.

Since a woman is wired for connection, she is usually the first to smell loss of relationship in the air. She feels the sting of rejection more poignantly. The rift between her and the man she loves—or the brother or son or friend she cares about—keeps her up at night. All of this gets mulled over in her larger hippocampus, which, apparently, comes equipped with additional circuitry for processing conflict. It's able to gather emotion and chew on it, much like a cow has an extra stomach that chews food before it's digested. (I had to overlook the offensive metaphor myself.)

So here we are, with a heightened awareness of relationships and a greater ability to put our feelings into words. We have more brain circuitry to sort through conflict and misunderstanding. You can see how this mix can become a volatile combination. *I'm upset, and I know why*. It can morph into the intensity of a talking fireball—or so it must appear to the unsuspecting male. Or as Louann Brizendine writes, "Though a woman is slower to act out of anger, once her faster verbal circuits get going, they can cause her to unleash a barrage of angry words a man can't match."[3]

You know how frustrating it can be when a man doesn't hear you—and how tempting it is to use harsh statements to get his attention. *I can't pound a man with my fists, but honey, I've got words that can cut him off at the knees*.

Whatever form "freaking out" takes in your relationship—be it biting words or stonewalling—that's the signal to stop. Time-out. Red flag on the field of play. The only thing worse than a bad conflict is letting it escalate. Real damage can be done to the relationship.

> *Whatever form "freaking out" takes in your relationship—be it biting words or stonewalling—that's the signal to stop.*

Calling a halt doesn't mean burying the thing in the backyard. No, calling a halt means that you make an appointment with each other to pick up this one issue (only this issue) in the next forty-eight to seventy-two hours. Believe me, you'll feel sane and clothed and back in your right mind by then.

It helps if you think of your relationship as a third party, a small child you must always protect. And so you watch each other's thermometer. When one of you is shutting down—or one of you is tossing out cutting phrases that sting upon entry—then stop the conversation at that point. And make an appointment.[4] Say something like, "After the kids are asleep, two days from now, we'll pick up this one issue of how we're going to handle my mother's visits."

I'm not implying that everything will be resolved in a neat package. (Remember the phrase *lifelong dialogue*?) But it's amazing the clarity and understanding that come with some sleep and some prayer. In between this heated discussion and the next time you talk, you get to have a life together. The issue is still there, waiting for you, in the walk-in closet. You'll get another chance.

Giving yourself a few days will allow you some time to unravel your own fears. That's important, since each of you is afraid of something. And your fear is what drives the stonewalling or the verbal jabs.

ANGER IN RELATIONSHIPS

Anger is the most seductive of all negative emotions. Unlike sadness, it's energizing. As such, it has addictive properties. Adrenaline and dopamine pour into the body, causing a temporary sense of empowerment. "Venting," then, can be followed by feelings of triumph and relief—except to the person vented upon.

Many myths surround our notions about anger. There's the idea that anger shouldn't be controlled. Venting, supposedly, brings catharsis. More accurately, though, anger breeds anger. Or as Proverbs 15:1 says, "A harsh word stirs up anger." Rarely does something productive happen between two people when their anger is allowed to drive the interaction. "The anger of man does not achieve the righteousness of God."[5]

The best thing to remember about anger is that it is always a secondary emotion. Always. So if we give ourselves some space—if we interview our anger—we will discover the fear or shame driving it. What you can, then, own and name, you can do something about. Naming what's really bothering you changes your conversation, and it changes the way you pray.

OVER-THE-TOP

In his best-selling book *Love and Respect*, Dr. Emerson Eggerichs relates the story of a huge guy who was stunned by his girlfriend's anger and what he perceived as an attack on him.

He was shocked that she was upset enough to say she hated him.

But the girlfriend was frustrated by his interpretation. "When I scream 'I hate you,' you should know I don't mean it. You are 6'9" and weigh 260 pounds, for goodness' sake. I do that because you can take it."

Eggerichs adds this commentary: "The truth is, however, a lot of men can't take it. No matter how big they may be physically, emotionally they are vulnerable to what sounds like contempt."[6]

Contempt is the operative word here (and women can't take it any better than men, by the way). In the world of human interaction, contempt is a blaring siren that makes your ears hurt. Contempt takes a number of forms:[7]

- Name-calling, labeling words like *turkey* or *witch* or *wimp* that communicate an attack on someone's character

- Harsh criticism, with extremist words sprinkled throughout: "You always . . ." or "You never . . ."

- A tone of voice that sounds condescending or demeaning

- Facial expressions like rolling one's eyes or shaking one's head in disgust and frustration

If a couple lets their arguments degenerate to this level, they can unravel a relationship in no time flat. It's toxic because it taps into the other person's shame, and shame is the hardest of all emotions to handle. Contempt confirms your worst self-doubts. *Sure enough, I've got an L for* Loser *taped to my forehead.* It's as though someone is seeing you up close, and is disgusted by what he sees.

Contempt is so potent in a relationship that elaborate studies of couples' communication can predict, with stunning accuracy, which couples will separate within four years—based on how many times in a fifteen-minute period a form of contempt is expressed.[8]

I belabor the notion of contempt for a number of reasons. For a man, contempt is synonymous with disrespect—the very opposite of the gas his car runs on. When there are critical remarks, smirks, and eye rolling, it's hard to contain the conflict in your walk-in closet. It can flat take over your relationship. And over time, it will tear the two of you to shreds.

REAPING THE BEST FROM CONFLICT

Quite honestly, though, I find it's very easy, as a woman, to express something laced with tiny drops of contempt, and hardly be aware of it. Or if I keep avoiding those black-eyed peas—if I repeatedly stuff something that's bothering me— then it may well squeak out in a weak moment in ways that feel like jabs.

When it does, it can seem quite justified. But I know those words, that look, and this tone of voice can dismantle the fabric of a relationship. In those moments, when there's too much criticism or my words have an edge, I need someone to hand me the equivalent of a blank legal pad. *Go write for fifteen minutes about what you're afraid of, Paula. And then pray about your fear. Only then should you put words to it.*

It's a scary thing, after all, to link your future with a man's. If he doesn't overcome a weakness, you are apt to feel the effect. If he steers his rowboat over some waterfall, you'll get wet too. Staring in the face of that possibility can transform a woman from being a man's best cheerleader into his difficult football coach or (just shoot me) his mother.

So that scared little girl in us must be tended to. The heat in a particular discussion tells a woman that she needs to let God doctor her own soul. I wonder if this was what the apostle Peter was talking about when he said that the path to wisdom and godliness lies right smack-dab through the field of your fears—and learning to trust God. Actually, the way Peter put it was that we would become daughters of Sarah if we did what was true and right without allowing fear to control us.[9]

This is why the lifelong dialogue of dealing with your fears and insecurities and pride—as they surface in conflicts with a man you love—pays big dividends all around. You start to deal with all those even-ifs. *Even if this boat goes*

> *The lifelong dialogue of dealing with your fears and insecurities and pride—as they surface in conflicts with a man you love—pays big dividends all around.*

over the waterfall, Jesus will still be there. No matter how solitary this conversation makes me feel, I am not alone.

Only Jesus has promised that he will never leave us or forsake us, and it's when we feel alone with someone we love that we are most reminded of that promise.[10]

Even though I am highly skilled at avoiding conflict, I realize that's a fruitless path. And though I'd love nothing more than an endless string of good times with a man, I know in my deep gut that we are each other's last, best chance to grow up.

There's really no way around it. Sometimes, you've just got to sit down and eat your peas.

Chapter 8

GETTING THROUGH

We must be reminded that the first condition for mutual
understanding is . . . the willingness to understand.
All the conversations of our world are,
for the most part, dialogues of the deaf.
—PAUL TOURNIER

Allan runs a commercial real estate firm in a Southern city where
streams of Yankees move, hoping to trade snow for azaleas.

He thinks about relationships with women, most notably
his wife, with the cool logic of a man who lives in a business
environment. His perspective is insightful. I suspect lots of
men see relationships this way.

"What you have to keep in mind with a woman," Allan told
me in a recent conversation, "is that you are always building up
equity—or withdrawing it from the account."

"Hm . . . equity in an account?" I asked him. "Tell me
more."

"Yes. Equity in an account. You make deposits in the
relationship—positive stuff, like remembering her birthday
and date nights and sharing some private jokes."

The idea, he said, is that it's a given there will be frustrating seasons, polarizing moments when it seems that one of you comes from Bosnia and the other, Serbia. You keep making deposits in the relationship because, inevitably, issues will arise that withdraw emotional capital.

A relationship in trouble is one where the accounts get overdrawn and fresh deposits are not being made.

All this strikes me as a particularly male way to think—like, maybe, they have ledgers in their brains I am unaware of. My own husband refers to "jelly beans in a jar," as though two actually exist out there in the universe with our names on them. If Stacy does something downright thoughtful, he might say, "Okay, are you counting that? It's worth two jelly beans in my jar." He's only half joking.

We all want what we do to count with the other person. We want what feels like love to us—to feel like love to them. It needs to matter because there are times in every relationship that try the soul. There are times when it feels as though you are standing on two cliffs over a great chasm and calling out to each other through a foghorn that can't be heard.

When Swiss psychologist Paul Tournier talked about the challenge men and women face, he likened this dialogue to the stumbling inadequacy you'd feel if you were marooned on an island with someone who doesn't speak English. You understand a bit of his Russian. He gets a few words of your English. Slowly you build a repertoire of shared phrases, the threads of understanding each other.

Given that you and this man see life a bit differently, how

do you wade through touchy topics? How do you get closer to reading from the same page?

WHERE TO BEGIN

When it comes to understanding each other, you and this man are trying to create an invisible, highly prized commodity called emotional safety. It's like actual space that allows you to walk through a hot-button topic. Or it's a bit of padding that helps you talk about hard things.

One way to think about emotional safety is to picture the two of you as kids in a sandbox. That's not too far off the mark. A man and a woman who've pledged some sort of troth are, indeed, in the same sandbox. For a long time. Keeping in mind the rules of the sandbox will help you make sustained progress in the delicate art of becoming a relational genius. Here are a few of those rules:

- *You have to share your toys.* You both have needs for affection and a kind word, even when you don't deserve them. Neither of you can hog all the good stuff. Take turns being crazy, so you aren't crazy on the same day.

- *You can't hit each other over the head with your dump truck.* No matter how upset you get with the person in your sandbox, you can't clobber him with words or manipulate his heart by withholding love and support.

- *You can't just, willy-nilly, pick up your marbles and go home.* The threat that one or the other of you will pack up and leave the playground in a huff is what keeps many a relationship from getting to the next level of intimacy.

I guess you could say that the rules of the sandbox are a starting point. They help create some basic parameters.

If there is one thing that helps you make progress with a man you're at odds with, it would be this: the freedom to explore an issue. When you investigate an issue with a man, you walk around it from new angles. You, literally, explore possibilities. If there's the potential of hurt and disagreement, that's what is most needed.[1]

> *If there is one thing that helps you make progress with a man you're at odds with, it would be this: the freedom to explore an issue.*

Sometimes, I make myself pretend I don't know this guy. This is not the man I've climbed in bed with for more than thirty years. Or it's not my son whose future hangs in the balance. This is not the brother I've known all my life. No, this man (like every person) is a walking mystery story filled with ghosts and untold tales.

All that's to say, if you explore possibilities, you come with a tad more humility. *Maybe there's something about him I still don't get.* You already know there are places in your relation-

ship where you don't feel understood. Sometimes it helps to
picture yourselves as two old friends in a coffee shop, talking.[2]
With a friend, you would step back ten paces and explore all
the angles.

Think, for a moment, about Laura from the previous chapter, who wanted more attention and help from her pharmacist
husband, Dan. If Laura wanted to pick up the question of
Dan's preoccupation with work and hobbies and how much
she feels she's carrying, her attempt to explore might sound
like this:

- "What feels so crucial to you about buying the next
  pharmacy now? What kind of possibilities do you
  see?"

- "How do you sense it's costing us something as a
  family—or us, as a couple?"

- "When do you feel the two of us have our best times
  together?"

- "What do you think is happening with me when
  you're off fishing or working?"

- "When can you tell I'm overwhelmed with all that's
  coming at me? What are the signals to you?"

Now, granted, all these questions could be asked as though
you were the prosecuting attorney in a courtroom trial and
this guy was on the witness stand. Or, they could be part of

the dialogue where you are genuinely exploring. "Help me understand what you're thinking."[3]

Sometimes, in a touchy conversation, I keep the word *explore* clicking in my brain, like it was on automatic replay. *Explore this, Paula. Explore, explore, explore.*

It keeps me circling, actively in search of the parts not easily seen. And if that doesn't work, then I let Proverbs poke its finger in my rib cage. I remind myself that the fool in Proverbs always has her (or his) mouth open, talking rather than listening.

> He who restrains his words has knowledge,
>> and he who has a cool spirit is a man of understanding.
> Even a fool, when he keeps silent, is considered wise;
>> when he closes his lips, he is considered prudent.[4]

WHAT TO AVOID AS YOU EXPLORE

There are two trip wires in a touchy conversation that either shut the whole thing down or escalate it beyond reason. The first is misinterpretation and the second, invalidation.[5]

MISINTERPRETATION

Misinterpretation occurs when one person consistently reads negative motives that aren't accurate into the actions of the other. Dan, for example, had so many irons in the fire trying to run multiple pharmacies that he'd occasionally get busy at work and forget to call Laura and tell her to not hold dinner for him.

When he forgot, though, Laura didn't view him as just a man who got preoccupied and forgot. She saw his absent-mindedness as evidence that he didn't care about her schedule or plans. The fact that he usually remembered to call was lost on her.

She read a motive into his actions that didn't fit his intention.

Have you ever been on the receiving end of someone else's negative interpretation? It's like you'll never get out of the doghouse. If you mess up, it's just more "evidence" for a conclusion the other person has already drawn. You feel defeated, as though you can't win.

The Bible says that malice is one of those things that, along with envy and hypocrisy, we want to let go of in our relationships.[6] And malice simply means imputing evil intent. It's making a more negative interpretation than fits the situation. The kicker is that if you hold up a negative lens, you'll see what you expect to see. Your assumptions will appear to be confirmed—even though they're wrong.

> *If you hold up a negative lens, you'll see what you expect to see. Your assumptions will appear to be confirmed—even though they're wrong.*

The best way to avoid misinterpretation is to check out your take on things. Don't just try to read a man's mind. Ask him where he's coming from. "What did you mean by that statement?" "What are you saying by that choice?" Be willing to hold open the possibility that there's another explanation than the one that may first appear to you.

INVALIDATION

We invalidate other people when we fail to validate their thoughts or feelings.

I often try to remind myself that I don't have to agree with a person to understand where he's coming from. It's possible to validate how someone feels and even commiserate a bit, without rubber-stamping his perspective.

Dan found this especially challenging. When he was gone or chronically preoccupied with work, Laura's complaint was that she felt like she was "right back there at fourteen, spinning plates, trying to keep a household going and meals prepared with a sick mother in her bedroom."

"That's just simply wrong," Dan would say. "I pull more than my weight around here. Stop comparing me to your mother."

Laura ached for him to validate how it could—at least—feel the same. No, Dan wasn't her sick mother. But Laura felt as alone and burdened as if he were. If Dan could understand how she felt (and it seemed no one ever had), she could get five steps closer to believing that, while she might have similar feelings, she wasn't stuck in the old story. She was a big girl now, and there were loads of possibilities. And Dan wasn't trying to leave her holding the bag while he went fishing.

Stopping long enough to validate the other person's

feelings, experience, or opin-
ions—even if you don't
totally agree—gives him permission to go beyond those
thoughts and feelings. It allows
new possibilities to be entertained. When we feel invali-
dated, we tend to stay stuck.
Then, unfortunately, we
remain two people on cliffs,

> *Stopping long enough
> to validate the
> other person's
> feelings, experience,
> or opinions . . .
> allows new possibilities
> to be entertained.*

shouting across a chasm through our very own foghorn that
can't be heard.

THE LANGUAGE OF UNDERSTANDING

One thing I appreciate about the Bible is the way God insists
that I get out of myself and into the mental and emotional
framework of another person. Even though what I really
want is to feel understood—more than I want to understand.
I often think of the apostle Paul's words: "With humility of
mind regard one another as more important than yourselves;
do not merely look out for your own personal interests, but
also for the interests of others."[7]

In practical terms, this is the language of empathy. *How
would I feel if I were living the story this man has lived?*

The catch is that if you've known a man a long time, you
may be too familiar with his life. It's all catalogued and labeled.
Yes, his dad left his mother for a gay relationship when he was

twelve. How, though, did it actually feel to have to find his way into being a man all by himself? What was it like to hear his mother crying in her bedroom and not be able to do anything to comfort her?

In Dan and Laura's life, she lived with the daily presence of Dan's famous father. The shopping center he built has their shared last name. Laura took this fame for granted, and over time the picture was denuded of its true meaning. But Dan's urgency to acquire a new pharmacy was directly connected to being the bookish boy who grew up in the shadows of a brother who played college football and a dad whose presence pulsated through any room he entered. Can she feel what that boy felt?

> *Empathy, for most men, is a slowly learned skill. It doesn't come naturally.*

The more she can feel what that boy feels, the easier she can talk to Dan, the man. "Honey, we don't need another pharmacy. We need a life together. You've done enough."

Of course, empathy flows two ways. Laura wants Dan to understand where she's coming from too. And empathy, for most men, is a slowly learned skill. It doesn't come naturally.

The language of empathy easiest for a man to hear is one that's expressed in word pictures. So when Laura says, "Look, if we keep going like this, I see myself as an old woman in a brown sweater with cats all around, while you're at the office or on a golf course," Dan may actually see what drives her.

Her words paint a picture of unattractive loneliness—which is her deepest fear.

Pictures are inherently more emotional. They reach a deeper place inside us. And for many men, the language of empathy they best understand is one expressed in images.

A CONSCIOUS STRUCTURE

Underneath every conversation with a man where you don't see eye to eye, an unspoken question lies waiting to be put into words. *What do you want?* You work hard to get deeper into each other's thoughts and feelings—to gain some perspective. *But what do you need to be different?* You can talk all day. *What, from your vantage point, would actually help the situation?*

What you want or need might seem obvious from where you sit. But most of the time, for a man—it's not.

If you could listen in on Dan and Laura's retake of that heated argument where she felt she had to handle everything alone—and he threw in the jab about not wanting to stay home and "hold her hand"—this is what you'd hear.

After some stumbling but genuine attempts to climb inside each other's heads, Laura finally says, "Look, honey, I'm not asking you to stay home and hold my hand. It saddens me that you'd even think that."

Dan starts to jump in with an explanation, but Laura holds up her hand. "No, wait," she says, "let me finish."

She reminds him of how they used to be more of a team. "We took on projects and did them together. I felt more comfortable—more at home—with you than any guy I'd ever known."

Dan looks like he feels a bit of comfort himself. Laura continues: "I need a partner. I want us to pick some activities we do together as a family—and some things we do, just the two of us—things I can count on. Even if it slows down other goals. It's just not the same without you."

Getting through to a man—or making progress as a couple—usually includes some basic aspects of what you see in this conversation. As I've mentioned, if you can translate anger into sadness, you will be heard more easily. Concern or sadness or grief flies beneath the radar of defensiveness when anger, often, just hits a wall.

You'll note that Laura translated her frustration into an actual request—one with legs on it. It was direct and clear. "I need a partner." She asked for something concrete and doable. She wasn't asking for the moon. She simply said, "Let's pick some activities we do as a family—or as a couple—and give them more priority."

A man often feels a woman is upset about something he can't get his hands around. She has a complaint, to be sure, but what is the request? Or in Freud's famous words, "What does a woman want?"

In Laura's words, there is a conscious structure to a difficult conversation. It's affectionately known by three descriptive words: *stroke, kick, stroke.* (It's better than it sounds). Some folks picture this like a sandwich that has two slices of bread with meat in the middle.

- *Stroke*. Share something you value or appreciate about this man—a good memory, a personal attribute. It might be an expression of empathy, like, "I know this is a miserable situation for you, and I wish I could make it better." Or as Laura said, she wasn't expecting Dan to stay home and hold her hand, but she felt more comfortable with him than anyone else.

- *Kick*. Make a specific request. Or tell him that you want something to be different. Or deliver a piece of news he may not like. "I just can't agree to that. I'm suggesting that we . . ."[8] Laura's "kick" to Dan was telling him she needed a partner even if they owned fewer pharmacies.

- *Stroke*. Try hard to return to something more positive. As Laura said, she and Dan were a team, and doing things without him just wasn't the same.

Now I'm the first to admit that, in a conversation with a man where something you value is at stake, it's hard as the dickens to not jump straight to the "kick" part. It takes a conscious effort to add in the strokes. But, oh, it helps. It's worth every bit of work to slow down and measure your words. Or as Proverbs says so well, "There is one who speaks rashly like the thrusts of a sword, but the tongue of the wise brings healing."[9]

YOUR OWN VULNERABILITY

When you wade into the choppy waters of a touchy conversation with a man you care about, it will stir the deepest stuff in your own heart. Inevitably. When you listen to the things that bother this man, it will remind you of the things bothering you. To ask for what you long for, to voice why something hurts—does it get more vulnerable than that?

In an honest moment, most women would say that this kind of vulnerability is the most naked experience they know. More vulnerable than sex. It's a soul-stretching exercise to try to hear a man deeply . . . and to feel heard yourself. There's no guarantee that you'll be well received or understood.

> *It's a soul-stretching exercise to try to hear a man deeply . . . and to feel heard yourself.*

That's why this sort of vulnerability can lead to so much spiritual growth in your life, and in his.[10] I find, over and over, that vulnerability forces me to cling to what I consider the deepest truth of my identity: I am, simply and actually, this woman Jesus loves. Being rooted there helps me take a few more risks with a man. And it helps me bear the possibility that he might not be a happy camper about something I've said or done.

Finally, it's important to remember that it may take some time before you know how a man processes the tangled threads between you. He has heard more of what you've said than may appear. Those thoughts, feelings, needs, or complaints get hauled back into a hidden compartment in his brain. There (and this is only a slight exaggeration), elves emerge and sort that pile of stuff while he sleeps. Watch and see what he does with it. Give him some time, as the elves are in no hurry.

Later, in a lighter moment over a latte in some coffee shop, you might ask, "Hey, what other thoughts have you had about that stuff we talked about?" It will be interesting to see what he says.

I wish the process of getting on the same page were more scientific. There are some real helps to understanding each other. But there's always a touch of mystery in the way it begins to happen, which is why loaded topics create a lifelong dialogue.

It takes time, but slowly you find yourself speaking a little more Russian. And he thinks your English makes a lot more sense.

Chapter 9

INTIMACY

You may not know it now, but you're gonna miss this.
—"YOU'RE GONNA MISS THIS,"
TRACE ADKINS

On Christmas Eve a few years back, I found myself browsing a small gift shop in my hometown in Virginia. I needed some last-minute stocking stuffers before I headed home to start the annual cooking marathon.

Carolee, the woman who owned this shop, was someone I'd known for years—not well, but well enough to know her husband had died that fall from esophageal cancer. He was only fifty-four.

I guess everyone else in town already had their stocking stuffers, because Carolee and I were the only two people in her shop when I made my purchases. As she handed me change, I asked her how she was doing. I told her how sorry I was to hear of Ken's death.

She responded almost philosophically, like a woman who had prepared herself for months for the unwanted inevitable.

This was her first big holiday without Ken. It would be

rough, she knew. So she was headed out of town to spend Christmas with an elderly aunt. With a half smile she said, "We can be lonely together."

Then she began to reminisce. "You know, Ken and I lived in a house at the lake with a huge picture window. In the late afternoons, we'd sit and watch the light fade over the water and we'd toast the sunset, grateful for the day."

We talked a few more minutes. I wished her a merry Christmas. And right before I left, she touched my arm and looked straight through me as she spoke four words like they were the most important gift I would receive that Christmas.

"Treasure the moments, Paula."

OVERCOMING THE MYTH

I, of all people, needed to hear those words. Actually, I need to tape those words to my bathroom mirror and nod assent to them every day. I am one of those women who gives too much thought to what ought to be and what should be. I'm big into if-onlys. Treasuring the moments in a relationship is a skill I am still learning.

Wanting what should be and could be is not the worst thing to be afflicted with; the momentum does carry you along. The problem is that, in close relationships, and especially in life with a man, if you ride the train of should-be and could-be too far, you will miss *what is*. And *what is* holds a surprisingly powerful amount of joy.

Intimacy is the holy grail of our day, and truthfully,

intimacy is not possible unless you can savor the small moments that come your way with a man. A good laugh over something crazy you heard that day. An early morning rendezvous before the kids wake up. Ten minutes of telling him why you nearly lost your mind in a meeting this afternoon. Intimacy is as fleeting and unpredictable as a butterfly, and frankly, it has little to do with peak experiences, like a trip to Italy. It's far more about enjoying the times that are simply, and rather sweetly, good.

> *In close relationships, and especially in life with a man, if you ride the train of should-be and could-be too far, you will miss what is.*

The enemy of our ability to savor the simple good is the myth that somewhere in the Cracker Jack box of relationships you are going to find your "soul mate." I know women who have been trying to make a man into the image of a soul mate longer than they've been coloring their hair. And I can't say I blame them. We are all victims of this myth. *If we solved conflict better, if we had the same interests, if you just talked more—something. There must be some key we've missed that would unlock the door to the complete-your-sentences world of soul mates.*

These days, when I hear the words *soul mate*, I am reminded of a favorite one-liner from comedian Bob Newhart, who said, "I make a motion that we all tell the truth."

The actual truth about soul mates is that, when all is said and done, only about one in ten relationships between a man and a woman enjoys such a natural closeness that they qualify for the title. Only one in ten couples *will ever* become "soul mates."

Another four in ten (roughly) have admirable, amicable relationships. They get along pretty well. Both people are mostly satisfied.

Then you start dropping below the baseline. Three in ten marriages are the union of two people who have to work hard at their relationship. That's not necessarily bad. Some couples do struggle harder to string good moments together.

And finally, one or two couples out of ten feel they are camped out on the frozen tundra of misery and their friends wonder how they make it.

It can be such a relief to break through the mirage of finding your soul mate. I heartily recommend it. In fact, I think it's worth every wrinkle on a woman's face to get past that myth. Then you actually have a fighting chance to enjoy the peculiarities of the man to whom you're attached. You are far less tempted to trade each other in at the used-spouse shop.

You aren't throwing out the more ordinary moments in search of the stellar ones. No, the simple good is actually quite good.

Good is beautiful.

INTIMACY IS BORN OF ACCEPTANCE

Here is a snippet of conversation of which any man and woman who've known each other longer than five years have a version. You may recognize something vaguely familiar in the push-and-pull of it.

We have a son who flies planes for a living and loves it. But sometimes, I get to thinking about that with Stacy and say, "Isn't it the oddest thing to have a child in the air all day, flying live people around? I mean, sometimes I wonder how he's landing those planes with all the summer storms I see on the weather map."

I have no visible proof of this, but I believe Stacy rolls his eyes on the inside as soon as I voice this particular worry. He will respond in shades of patience or impatience, depending on when he last ate or how well he slept. "Paula, Brady has received the best training out there. He is a good pilot."

As if choreographed, I'll say something like, "But honey, we knew him when he was three years old."

And Stacy will respond on cue: "You've got to let this boy be a man, honey. He'll do fine. Really, he will do fine."

Now, I know, deep down, that I'm not crazy to worry. And Stacy knows that no man needs a fretting mother—especially a guy who flies planes. But our conversation strikes a nerve each time because, really, it's a reflection of a fundamental difference between us that hasn't changed since the day we met—though we probably thought it would.

I still think this man sees through rose-colored glasses.

He thinks I overreact to worst-case scenarios that won't happen.

Like I say, every couple who hangs together has a version of this—a set of differences that doesn't change much over time. A set of differences that must be accepted and somehow accommodated.

There is some fine irony in the reality that, most likely, what bugs the living daylights out of you about the man in your life is the very thing that made you want to merge your gene pool with his to begin with. What I loved and still love about Stacy is his optimism and his stability. And what attracted him to me was that I didn't just think about life—I felt it as well.

> *Some of this man's weaknesses and flaws are the front door through which you enter and experience the love of God, which is the best of all loves.*

All of this makes for the basic need to accept a man in the package he comes in, and truthfully, a little more acceptance goes a long way toward treasuring the small moments that make up what anyone calls intimacy.

My growing suspicion is that when God sees a couple with a commitment to him and to each other, he values the holes in the relationship as much as the fabric itself. What is missing is usually missing for a reason. From God's perspective, some of the traits you feel are lacking in this man are going to be the occasion of your own growth in ways you can scarcely imagine. And perhaps you'd never go there if you didn't feel a painful longing. Some of this man's weaknesses and flaws are the front door through which you enter and experience the love of God, which is the best of all loves.

That's not to say any of this is easy and you don't wish, perhaps, that it were otherwise. It is not easy. But when did easy ever take us where we truly wanted to go?

Sometimes, when I'm in search of more acceptance in a relationship, I flip through the pages of the New Testament until I find Paul's parting words to the Romans. It's the very thing I need to hear in any close relationship—most significantly, with the man in my life. Paul writes about accepting another person for the most telling reason: Christ accepted me.

> May the God of endurance and encouragement grant you to live in such harmony with one another . . . that together you may with one voice glorify the God and Father of our Lord Jesus Christ. Therefore *welcome one another as Christ has welcomed you,* for the glory of God.[1]

To welcome someone is to accept him in the same spirit that Christ has welcomed me, knowing there's a cost involved. Accepting each other, weaknesses included, is just the place where God's glory shines through.

INTIMACY IS IN THE MOMENT

Toward the end of Bette Davis's life, she looked back on her career as an actress—and especially on her four attempts at marriage. "In selecting husbands, I confused muscle with strength," she said. "I was a person who couldn't make divorce work. For me, there's nothing lonelier than a turned-down toilet seat."[2]

Perhaps we all have our own versions of the things that remind us we aren't alone. That there is a man present. Maybe it's a deep voice on the end of the phone. Or a particular sort of advice that doesn't sound like our own perspective rehashed. The smell of male sweat on a hot afternoon. The safe feeling of arms that are stronger than ours.

A big part of intimacy in a relationship hangs on our openness to appreciate what is not like us. Much of having an intimacy that lasts is about enjoying a man's otherness.

I will never forget a conversation I had with a guy who was trying to put his marriage back together after an affair he was sorry he'd had. Given his remorse, how did he ever let himself get sucked into an affair? I asked.

He thought about the question for a long time. "It wasn't the sex," he said. He seemed pretty sure of that.

"Okay, then what was it?"

"Well, I used to go to a restaurant with her, and sometimes she'd reach over and put her hand on my arm. We'd laugh at something funny. She just simply enjoyed being with me."

I'm not trying to excuse an affair—not even the least little bit. Yet I realize that this man is voicing something right at the heart of what most feels like love to us, man or woman. *The pleasure of feeling enjoyed by someone.* Hardly anything feels so intimate.

Think, for a minute, of this particularly beautiful Old Testament picture of the love of God. What moves you when you read these words?

> The LORD your God is in your midst,
> a mighty one who will save;
> he will rejoice over you with gladness;
> he will quiet you by his love;
> he will exult over you with loud singing.[3]

These are not the words of a reluctant lover. We who have failed him are—of all things!—being sung over. Celebrated. Loved. We are being enjoyed by the living God.

In a tiny but very real way, what feels like love between two human beings is mostly a string of moments in which you feel enjoyed. Again, intimacy means letting yourself enjoy a man (and hoping for the same) even though your lives are always in flux and neither of you is fixed and you may never quite agree on how often you should eat out.

> *What feels like love between two human beings is mostly a string of moments in which you feel enjoyed.*

If you wait until the package is complete, you'll miss all the moments in between.

YOU MAKE YOU HAPPY

One of the secret aspects of staying close has to do with how we see the nature of happiness. If we hitch our sense of feeling good onto the coattails of someone else—especially a man—then, generally speaking, we'll feel anything but good. The weight of carrying someone else's emotional life can pull any relationship down.

This is a subtle dynamic in our lives as women. After all, the structure of our brains means that we feel things like sadness and anxiety more than men do. We feel them more deeply. We feel them longer. It's the most natural inclination in the world to want those closest to you to make things better.

But happiness, by which I mean that day-to-day sense of feeling good, is a strange thing.[4] Most of us are just about as happy as we choose to be. Given that reality, there are two basic questions that always need to be near at hand in any woman's life:

- "Okay, honey, what would help?"

- "What do you actually need?"

These questions should be spoken with compassion. After all, you may take care of small children and elderly parents, the newly divorced woman at the office—perhaps half your neighborhood. So you must be able to sit yourself down, like a good mother who would pat a child on the knee, and say,

"Honey, what do *you* actually need . . . in this moment or this season of your life?"

Those two questions usually lead a woman to a growing repertoire of small things that make a big difference over time. Here are some of the ones I hear most often:

- More exercise

- A quiet coffee shop with a good book and a couple of hours where no one asks me for anything

- A day alone with God

- Dinner and a movie, just the two of us

- A warm bath with candles before I go to bed

My personal favorite is to fix a cup of tea in a china cup so I can sit on my back porch and watch the sunlight filter through Carolina pine trees.

Now, I realize (and you realize) that when you entertain this question, the simple things that come to your mind will not make all things new. Though you get more exercise, your husband might still be looking for a job and your grandchildren are still moving to California. It's just that *you* will be in a slightly better place.

I try to keep in mind the words of Moses, spoken to people (like us) who were worn and weary wanderers: "Only give heed to yourself and keep your soul diligently, so that you do not forget the things which your eyes have seen."[5]

In other words, it's not self-centered to ask yourself, "What is the state of my own soul? What keeps me alive on the inside in the midst of all life throws my way? How do I stay tuned to the things God is showing me?"

When we see happiness as something that's primarily determined from within us, something rather magical happens in close relationships—especially with the men in our lives. For if there's anything men resist with a passion, it's being held hostage to what feels (to them) like the impossible task of keeping a woman happy. The dance of intimacy comes to a halt.

Here is a story we've all lived at one time or another. It's universal, though the particulars vary. Woman feels down (quite a bit). Life feels overwhelming to her. Man runs his own business, but he notices his wife is not in the best of moods. She would like for them to go away for the weekend, but she wants him to plan it. Only this man is not a planner. He lives by the code of spontaneity.

An open weekend comes along, and he suggests an interesting place to go. But his wife is feeling rather rotten. She can't imagine inventing the weekend from scratch. She turns him down. He feels defeated. He gets even busier at work.

What a vicious cycle this kind of thing can be. If, however, your happiness and my happiness are under our own column on the emotional ledger, then we will approach life differently. If what you need is a weekend out of town and this man is amenable, and you like those weekends planned, then plan away. And when you get there, let yourself receive it as a gift. Let in the joy.

When a woman does the things she needs to do to get to a happier place, she often discovers that the man in her life mysteriously begins to move in her direction. Maybe she takes an art class or gets a new haircut. He probably has no idea why, exactly, she's in a better frame of mind. She just feels safer, a bit more inviting. He may even interpret her better mood as respect and appreciation for him! Whatever it is, she is not (yet) one more woman he is not man enough to please.

> *Most of us are, indeed, about as happy as we choose to be. And we feel closer to the men in our lives when our happiness comes from our own sane choices.*

It is a well-kept secret, hidden in the fine print of our longing for closeness and intimacy: most of us are, indeed, about as happy as we choose to be. And we feel closer to the men in our lives when our happiness comes from our own sane choices.

SOMETHING GREATER HAPPENING

I want to leave you with an apologetic for staying emotionally engaged with the man in your life over the long haul. (It's the only way to gather a collection of moments to treasure, actually.) This is the basis for intimacy, but it is easier said than done.

In a relationship with the man you love (or a brother or a

son), two realities are present. There's the obvious good of what this man brings to your life (and you to his). And there's also a gap between the obvious good and what you wish he supplied. Every pairing has both—the obvious good and the gap.

Sometimes, in the face of the gap, a woman gives up. She scratches a man off her dance card. And while she may still do his laundry or go to church with him, her hopes and dreams and fears and feelings get tucked so far out of sight even she can't find them. I know the temptation. I think every woman does.

What keeps a woman from staying in a cynical, shut-down place is actually not the man himself. It's a hopeful expectancy that somehow, when you least expect it, you will stumble on small pockets of the sheer goodness of God in this relationship. If God is present, there are *always* more possibilities than meet the eye. Or as is said in a quote I have loved for many years, "There is nothing small that God is in."[6]

> *Grace pours into a relationship as we take ten steps back:* something greater is happening here than the two of us.

Grace pours into a relationship as we take ten steps back: *something greater is happening here than the two of us.* God has purposes for your lives together that are greater than your individual comfort or ease. It is worth the work of relationship. A man and a woman together, albeit imperfectly, reflect the glory of God in ways nothing else in creation can.

More than all the how-to books on my shelf, what grounds me in sanity in a relationship with a man is the model of Jesus.

> *We do, indeed, live not just for our own well-being but also for the redemption of the other person.*

Simply the example of Christ. The trail he blazed for us is one of self-emptying love—not that Jesus obliterated himself or lacked a self to give. No. He poured himself out for our good. And any man and woman who make it together, make it no other way than by believing that out of the small humilities and sacrifices of relationship, God will bring life.

We do, indeed, live not just for our own well-being but also for the redemption of the other person.

In the big picture of your relationship, you are experiencing in your best moments with this man some aspect of God that, otherwise, you would know only as a concept. It is this man's strength or courage or care that gives you a tiny peek behind the veil.

And yet, he is only a man—as flawed and dependent on God's mercy as you and I are. Sometimes what we experience of God comes in spite of this man . . . in the holes of the fabric of our joint humanity.

I try to remind myself often that Stacy and I are, mostly, two sinners who stumbled into each other one summer . . . and then began to walk the same path. And while God is there on the trail and we are not doing this alone, still the simple reality is that neither of us will be made whole or holy in this life.

I wonder, sometimes, if we won't run into each other on the other side and say, "Oh, I always thought this is who you'd become. Lo and behold, now you are."

Only the remembrance of the big picture—the whole story—will let us treasure the moments now, sweet and bittersweet.

AFTERWORD

All these men in your life. Line up their faces again in your mind—the ones you love, the ones who drive you crazy. Let me say it one more time for both of us: men aren't just women with big feet and beards. They are *other*. Relating to them is a daily immersion in another world, at once familiar and yet far away, full of longing and pleasure and the sheer effort of calling across that gulf that separates you.

Of all these men, there will be a handful who *really* matter to you, and you will long for something, everything, anything that will make the gap smaller.

I hope I've been the credible voice of another woman in your life, saying in so many words, "Honey, you aren't imagining the gap." After thirty years of the great androgynous experiment, neuroscience (brains wired to computers) is confirming what you intuitively knew: men and women are two distinctive genders, and we cannot be made to look at life the same. *Cannot.* Not in the rain and not on the train, as Dr. Seuss would have said. As much as we want to be in total control of our fate—alas, gender determines much beyond our reach. We are not our own Maker.

It is God who reveals himself in a mystery so great it takes two genders to even give us a peek.

That reality will always be the backdrop to your quest to understand men, especially the important men in your life. It breeds a sort of natural curiosity. *I wonder how this feels inside the skin of this guy.* It takes a bit of humility to wonder, to realize just how different it could feel. Maybe, just maybe, what you're seeing is the way men do things in the land-of-the-other. For reasons that make sense—there, at least.

I belabor this because the simple desire to understand will carry you where you want to go in most relationships with men. What you don't yet know is really more important than what you think you know. Or as the book of Proverbs says so well, God gives wisdom as you "[apply] your heart to understanding" and "call out for insight," like a woman in search of a hidden treasure.[1]

It's odd but true: the quest to understand and the awareness that you don't yet know are the basis for being a "relational genius," as though you have to go to Detroit to get to Paris. Becoming a relational genius is mostly about being the bright woman you are with a growing insight into where this guy's coming from. With understanding, it will come to you—the words you need to say or the golden silence. The courage to stand your ground. Or the mercy of forgiving and being forgiven.

With understanding, you will be able to face your own fears too. And nothing quite so excavates those as a close relationship with a man you love.

The relationship itself will always and only be the small story set inside the great story. God loves you. Christ died for you. This is the never-ending love story, the tale of the ages. Occasionally, some man's face will mirror that reality to you afresh. And sometimes it will be a man's absence or his failure that will pull you closer to the One who never leaves.

Whatever brilliance in relationships we achieve is borne of the humility of all we don't yet understand . . . and the certainty of a Love that transcends even the best of human love.

PRAYING FOR THE MAN IN YOUR LIFE

What you want most to see happen in a man's life, only God can do.

When you are praying for a man, especially if he's your husband, it helps to anchor those prayers in Scripture. And there are some incredible passages from which to pray.

WISDOM

> Make me know Your ways, O LORD;
> teach me Your paths.
> Lead me in Your truth and teach me,
> for You are the God of my salvation;
> for You I wait all the day.
>
> —Psalm 25:4–5

STRENGTH

> . . . for he was marvelously helped until he was strong.
> —2 Chronicles 26:15

God is our refuge and strength,

a very present help in trouble.

Therefore we will not fear, though the earth should
change,

and though the mountains slip into the heart of the
sea . . .

—Psalm 46:1–2

REFUGE

Each will be like a refuge from the wind

and a shelter from the storm,

like streams of water in a dry country,

like the shade of a huge rock in a parched land.

—Isaiah 32:2

HUMILITY

All of you, clothe yourselves with humility toward one
another, for GOD IS OPPOSED TO THE PROUD, BUT GIVES
GRACE TO THE HUMBLE. Therefore humble yourselves
under the mighty hand of God, that He may exalt you at
the proper time, casting all your anxiety on Him, because
He cares for you.

—1 Peter 5:5–7

FRIENDS

He who walks with wise men will be wise,

but the companion of fools will suffer harm.

—Proverbs 13:20

BOLDNESS

The wicked flee when no one is pursuing,
but the righteous are bold as a lion.

—Proverbs 28:1

PURITY OF HEART

One thing I have asked from the LORD, that I shall
seek:
that I may dwell in the house of the LORD all the days
of my life,
to behold the beauty of the LORD
and to meditate in His temple.

—Psalm 27:4

A COOL SPIRIT

Like a city that is broken into and without walls
is a man who has no control over his spirit.

—Proverbs 25:28

There is one who speaks rashly like the thrusts of a
sword.
But the tongue of the wise brings healing.

—Proverbs 12:18

Appendix B

UNDERSTANDING *THIS* MAN

Here are some questions to keep in mind as you seek to understand the man in your life. Some of them may even be appropriate conversation starters for the two of you:

WHERE HE HAS COME FROM
If he could repeat one era or one experience in his past, what would that be? Why?

If he could delete one era or experience, what would that be? Why?

When did he first feel (or ever feel):

     . . . like the odd duck?
     . . . a sense of rejection or failure?
     . . . the triumph of accomplishment?
     . . . a longing for something to be different?
     . . . lonely or afraid?

What kind of affirmation did he feel from his dad? What does he wish his father had said to him—or he had said to his father?

When he was growing up, when was he most aware of God? How did God get his attention . . . his heart? Or in what way might he wish he'd discovered God earlier?

When did he first know that his parents weren't perfect? What kind of impact did that have on him?

What did he always secretly wish he'd had the opportunity to do . . . but he never got the chance?

What experiences most made him want to hide?

What advice would he give a younger version of himself?

HOW HE SEES HIS OWN LIFE

When does he feel or has he felt the most free to be himself? And why?

What are the words he most longs to hear? What are the words he most fears hearing? What words have been said to him that have been life-giving?

What communicates respect to him? What are the times in his life when he felt particularly respected or disrespected?

How does his choice of work he loves—or the work he believes he would love—give you clues to his temperament and his abilities? (For example, a podiatrist tends to be drawn to the tangible and concrete results.)

Where does his greatest passion and motivation lie: in shaping ideas, in changing/leading/helping people, or in building/creating some*thing*? How has that motivation been seen in his past? What expression does he want that to take in his future?

From his standpoint, what purpose does a particular hobby or sport serve in his life?

HOW HE SEES YOUR RELATIONSHIP

When does he feel closest to you? And what makes him feel most estranged?

What seems better in his life to him when he's happy about his sexual life with you?

What kind of emotional triggers is he unable to tolerate (for example, he exits the room, diverts the conversation, cracks a joke, gets angry)?

What has been the hardest thing for him to forgive?

What does he secretly wish the two of you did together?

When does he feel respected? What causes him to feel disrespect?

HIS DREAMS FOR THE FUTURE

If he died now, would he feel that God was pleased with his life?

Is there some kind of new endeavor he senses God has for him in the future?

What is his toleration for risk, financially and in relationships, and how does it differ from yours?

He could "die happy" if he did what?

He'd feel the most sense of loss if he never got the chance to do what?

What does it look like for the two of you to dream together?

RELATIONAL GENIUS GUIDE

I tend to believe that we only feel the true impact of under-standing as we write and talk and pray about something we're learning. So this section is designed with the hope that it will provide you—or a group—a few extra moments to consider the great opportunity of understanding men better. Of under-standing yourself better. And of understanding God's desire to reflect his beauty and truth through your lives together.

Please know that I'm a big proponent of marriage. I realize that lots of women reading these questions will be thinking of their husbands. But many of us aren't married. We have fathers, sons, brothers, good male friends, and would-be, could-be, might-be husbands (boyfriends). And a huge number of these reflective questions can be applied to a relationship with any man who really matters to us—not just a husband. Feel free to think broadly through your life as you reflect on this material.

Remember, the point is not that you and I would merely have more satisfying, less-stressed relationships with men if we just understood them better. That will happen, but it's the icing on the cake.

The real good is that you and I will walk through our lives

with a more breathtaking awe of a God so amazing that it takes both genders to even have a peek at his beauty.

So give yourself some time and space to think and feel—to write and pray and talk to other women about the endlessly fascinating topic of *men*.

Chapter 1

UNDERSTANDING YOUR INFLUENCE

1. What in your personal relationships with men reminds you that they are coming from a different place and that they value different things?

2. What's wonderful about those differences, and what is frustrating?

3. Think about Hillary's words as she walked out the door: "Honey, you're going to miss me when I'm gone." When are you reminded of the worth and importance that you bring to a man? What would it mean for *you* to value that more?

4. In the garden of Eden, God saw how much Adam needed someone. "I will make a helper suitable for him," God said.

Metaphorically speaking, Adam did handstands when he saw
the woman God created for Adam's side. "This is now bone of
my bone and flesh of my flesh," he said. Read Genesis 2:18–25,
a passage full of relational meaning. What does this passage say
to you about what you mean or what you are meant to mean
to a man?

5. Eve's presence in Adam's life brings life. In your relationships with men, how do you bring life, beauty, hope, possibility, or support?

6. The book of Proverbs ends with what it means to a man to
have a good woman as his wife:

> An excellent wife, who can find?
> for her worth is far above jewels.
> The heart of her husband trusts in her,
> and he will have no lack of gain.
> She does him good and not evil
> all the days of her life. (Proverbs 31:10–12)

If you are married, what do these words say to you about
your importance to your husband? What does it look like in

your relationship to do this man good and to have the trust of his heart?

7. Part of the insight you've been given as a woman also helps you understand the man in your life. Look at the categories listed on pages 10–13. Which one or two descriptions fit him best—and why? Does he agree? How does this play out in your relationship?

Chapter 2

WHAT MEN DO

1. How do the men in your life express the "drive to do"? What are the best and worst aspects of that as it affects you?

2. The distinctions in men and women are especially evident after Adam and Eve disobeyed God, in what's commonly known as the Curse. Note the burden that Adam (and all men) carry through their lives:

> Then to Adam [God] said, "Because you have listened to the voice of your wife, and have eaten from the tree about which I commanded you, saying, 'You shall not eat from it';
>
> > Cursed is the ground because of you;
> > in toil you will eat of it all the days of your life.
> > Both thorns and thistles it shall grow for you;
> > and you shall eat the plants of the field;
> > by the sweat of your face
> > you will eat bread,
> > till you return to the ground,

because from it you were taken;

for you are dust,

and to dust you shall return. (Genesis 3:17–19)

How does this reality play out in the work life of the man you love? What does it mean for you to appreciate what he has to do to beat back the thorns and thistles?

3. A woman can be threatened by the power behind a man's strength, and yet, she may just as deeply hate his passivity. Here is a crucial question: what does it look like in your life to welcome a man's strength—to invite, celebrate, and even insist on it—and still be able to say no to whatever might be an abuse of his power? How does your relationship with Christ make you more able to invite a man's strength without canceling out your own?

4. In what tangible, active forms of "doing" does the man in your life express love? Which do you hear best and which do you tend to discount?

5. Around this question of a man's "drive to do," we can have a variety of responses. Here are some examples:

a. I take for granted the way this man goes to a job he may or may not like every day, takes seriously his need to provide, and does stuff for me; but he doesn't say much.

b. I am frustrated because this man gives the best of himself to everyone else all day and comes home to me . . . used up.

c. I feel disappointed when this man doesn't do—when he lets things fall through the cracks.

Pick one of these common pitfalls or reactions and write (or talk) about how it plays out in your relationship with a man.

6. In what way did this chapter give you a window into the world your man inhabits, and what kind of renewed appreciation does that give you?

Chapter 3

WHY MEN HURT

1. What are the cracks in the armor of the men in your life that give you insight into the hurt they carry inside? Do they strike a note of empathy, anger, or sadness in you . . . or something else—and why?

2. Name one thing from this chapter that made you more aware of the challenge of being a man.

3. When does the man in your life struggle most with the question of "Am I man enough?" How does that affect your relationship? What, on a personal level, seems to help?

4. In this man's story, what insights have you been given into the back room of his memories—experiences marked by fear,

guilt, shame, or loss? What parts would you like to understand more deeply?

5. What are a couple of questions that, in the right moment, might take you deeper into the thoughts and feelings of the man in your life?

6. The more you understand about a man's inner life, the greater the potential of a strong relationship. Below are some classic "one another" passages from the New Testament. Considering that this man is also your brother in Christ, these passages can powerfully shape your relationship for good.

Read these passages and write or talk about how you would apply them in your relationship.

Accept one another, just as Christ also accepted us to the glory of God. (Romans 15:7)

Be kind to one another, tender-hearted, forgiving each other, just as God in Christ also has forgiven you. (Ephesians 4:32)

Let us hold fast the confession of our hope without wavering . . . and let us consider how to stimulate one another to love and good deeds. (Hebrews 10:23–24)

Chapter 4

HOW MEN CHANGE

1. With the man in your life, how does his process of change look different than yours? Are there any subtle changes you sense you might have missed?

2. Has he ever hit a wall? What influences have accounted for the greatest changes in his life—or in yours?

3. Is there an area where you need to help him be a better man by saying, "This doesn't work for me"?

4. "Most men don't know how powerful they are." What would it look like in your relationship to reflect back to this man that

he has what it takes—that you value the good he brings into your life?

5. In the Old Testament, God chose David to be Israel's king, yet his jealous brothers dismissed him and Saul tried to kill him on multiple occasions. This was God's way of transforming David from a shepherd boy to a king who served his people and who served God well. A number of psalms record David's thoughts as he struggled with his circumstances. Read some of these below:

I will cry to God Most High,
to God who accomplishes all things for me.
He will send from heaven and save me;
He reproaches him who tramples upon me. (Psalm 57:2–3)

I sought the LORD, and He answered me,
and delivered me from all my fears. (Psalm 34:4)

I cried out to You, O LORD;
I said, "You are my refuge,
my portion in the land of the living.
Give heed to my cry,
for I am brought very low . . .
Bring my soul out of prison,
so that I may give thanks to Your name." (Psalm 142:5–7)

How do you see this process being played out in your man's life—or how do David's words motivate you to pray for the man in your life?

6. When this man goes through a difficult time, you will feel the effect. There are many places in Scripture to turn for encouragement. Here are two examples:

> We were burdened excessively, beyond our strength, so that we despaired even of life . . . so that we would not trust in ourselves, but in God who raises the dead; who delivered us from so great a peril of death, and will deliver us, He on whom we have set our hope. (2 Corinthians 1:8–10)

> Friends, when life gets really difficult, don't jump to the conclusion that God isn't on the job. Instead, be glad that you are in the very thick of what Christ experienced. This is a spiritual refining process, with glory just around the corner. (1 Peter 4:12–13 MSG)

How do these verses impact the way you ride out difficult times in your own life—or as you walk through life with a man?

Chapter 5

EXPECTATIONS

1. This chapter mentions the absence of cultural influences shaping boys into men these days. From what you've observed, how does our culture domesticate men, idolize their sexuality, parody them, or view them as a threat? How have these cultural views affected what you expect from a man?

2. The prophet Isaiah notes that when a culture turns away from God, men tend to withdraw and abdicate their strength as men. Read his words below:

> When a man lays hold of his brother in his father's house, saying,
> "You have a cloak, you shall be our ruler,
> and these ruins will be under your charge,"
> He will protest on that day, saying,
> "I will not be your healer,
> for in my house there is neither bread nor cloak;
> You should not appoint me ruler of the people." . . .
> O My people! Their oppressors are children,

and women rule over them.

O My people! Those who guide you lead you astray
and confuse the direction of your paths. (Isaiah
3:6–7, 12)

How do you see Isaiah's words evidenced in our culture?
In your own relationships with men?

3. What God has put in a man is there to be hoped for, called
upon, and celebrated. In your personal relationships with
men, what causes you to expect too little? What causes you to
expect too much?

4. Sometimes, especially in Christian circles, women succumb
to the notion that love means never expecting anything. The
emphasis is on loyalty and being accommodating (which has
its place). Yet when you think of the responsibility God places
on men and the sacrificial, Christlike love He calls them to,
how would that reality inform what a woman would hope for
or expect from a man?

5. Genesis 3:16 records the curse that fell upon women as the result of disobeying God: "Your desire will be for your husband, and he will rule over you." A paraphrased interpretation of that curse might sound something like, "You will always want more from a man than you can get." In other words, disappointment of some sort is nearly a guarantee.

Given that reality, in what way(s) has God met you as you have been disappointed by a man—or in what way(s) do you need for him to meet you?

6. You can only live with expectation and hope in your relationships if you can also embrace vulnerability. Let's look at this pattern in Christ, who was introduced by John the Baptist in this way: "Behold, the Lamb of God who takes away the sin of the world!" (John 1:29). When Christ returns, he will be known as the Lamb who conquers (Revelation 17:14 ESV). Consider a couple of instances of the manner in which Jesus lived this in his closest relationships:

> Jesus, knowing that the Father had given all things into His hands, and that He had come forth from God and was going back to God, got up from supper, and laid aside His garments; and taking a towel. . . . He poured water into the basin, and began to wash the disciples' feet and to wipe them with the towel. (John 13:3–5)

He said to them, "My soul is deeply grieved, to the point of death; remain here and keep watch with Me." And He went a little beyond them, and fell on His face and prayed, saying, "My Father, if it is possible, let this cup pass from Me; yet not as I will, but as You will." And He came to the disciples and found them sleeping, and said to Peter, "So, you men could not keep watch with Me for one hour?" (Matthew 26:38–40)

How do you see the vulnerability of Christ shown in these passages? What motivates you or encourages you along that same path?

7. Write (or talk) about one place in your life where vulnerability or disappointed expectations brought you something richer with God—and eventually, even something richer with this man.

Chapter 6

RESPECT

1. God tells a man to love his wife as Christ loved the church and gave himself up for her (Ephesians 5:25). But to a woman, the instruction is equally clear: "The wife must see to it that she respects her husband" (v. 33). Even though the context is marriage, the insight is universal. *Love* tends to be a woman's greatest need, and *respect* is usually a man's. Name a few ways in which you are conscious of offering the man or men in your life respect . . . and a few ways in which you wish you could offer more.

2. Given that every man disappoints and even the best men fail to merit respect at times, it's important to realize that respect is rooted in something deeper than his immediate behavior. Look at this bedrock verse in Genesis: "God created man in His own image, in the image of God He created him; male and female He created them" (1:27).

How would you put into your own words the transcendent reality that makes respect, in some form, always possible?

3. *Sex and the City* is a TV series and a movie that supposedly portrays how the sophisticated woman handles the men in her life. The fundamental tenet is that a smart woman no longer requires a man for status or a paycheck. Even her relational needs are met by other women.

It's amazing how easily this attitude infiltrates our relationships with men. It's easier to not need than to need and feel disappointed. How have you come to see your need of the man or men in your life as a foundational aspect of respect?

4. In many ways, *respect* is close to *honor*. To honor a man is to realize his value as a man and his weight in your life. Consider how clear the apostle Paul's words are: "Let love be without hypocrisy. Abhor what is evil; cling to what is good. Be devoted to one another in brotherly love; give preference to one another in honor" (Romans 12:9–10).

How do you honor the importance and the value of the man you love—or the men who really matter to you?

5. When does your effort to respect a man unearth your own fears? And why?

6. How does a woman's willingness to take a difficult stand with the man she loves—because it's right and she believes better of him—actually reflect her respect for him? When have you done that, or when could you see yourself doing that?

Chapter 7

CONFLICT

1. What extended dialogues are part of the undercurrent of your relationship with the man in your life?

2. When you think of conflict as a lifelong dialogue that you keep in your walk-in closet and pull out to sort through, on occasion, does that discourage you—or does it take the pressure off? And why?

3. Sometimes in a relationship, it's more important to note what went right in an interaction, rather than focus on the times you'd call failures. Think of a time when the two of you were able to deal with an issue rationally, make some progress, and then put it back in the walk-in closet and have a life together.

Now list everything you can think of, big and small, that made this interaction work well. (For example, things like, you'd had sex the night before, he looked at you when you

talked to him, you nodded frequently to indicate you understood his point, you prayed after you talked, and so on.)

Talk with him about the things you've written down. What
are the most important elements to bring into your next challenging conversation?

4. In a conflict that persists, there are two adults and two scared
kids in the room. In your relationship, if you put a microphone
in front of each kid, what would he or she be saying? What is
he or she so afraid of?

Now check this out with him. Would he agree—or would
he amend those words in some way . . . and why?

5. How would you each speak to the other person's fears?
What words of reassurance do you need to hear? What words
does he need to hear?

6. Think of a time when anger, contempt, or stonewalling
drove or accompanied your interaction with the man in your

life. Take a few moments in the cool light of day to assess the damages. What havoc did it cause?

7. Here are three gold-standard verses (among many) that have the power to dramatically affect the way we interact with others. Rewrite each in your own words.

> Walk in a manner worthy of the calling with which you have been called, with all humility and gentleness, with patience, showing tolerance for one another in love. (Ephesians 4:1–2)

> Do nothing from selfishness or empty conceit, but with humility of mind regard one another as more important than yourselves; do not merely look out for your own personal interests, but also for the interests of others. (Philippians 2:3–4)

> Speaking the truth in love, we are to grow up in all aspects into Him who is the head, even Christ. . . . Therefore, laying aside falsehood, SPEAK TRUTH EACH ONE of you WITH HIS NEIGHBOR, for we are members of one

another. BE ANGRY, AND yet DO NOT SIN; do not let the
sun go down on your anger, and do not give the devil an
opportunity. (Ephesians 4:15, 25–27)

8. Look again at what you've written. If you applied the most
appropriate verse to the situation you mentioned in question 6,
what would you do differently?

Chapter 8

GETTING THROUGH

1. The story at the beginning of this chapter underscores the need to continue to make "deposits" in a relationship. Consider this passage from Psalm 37. How would you apply this to your relationship?

> Trust in the LORD and do good;
> dwell in the land and cultivate faithfulness. . . .
> Commit your way to the LORD,
> trust also in Him, and He will do it.
> He will bring forth your righteousness as the light
> and your judgment as the noonday. (vv. 3, 5–6)

2. What threatens your sense of emotional safety in this relationship? What threatens his?

3. If you picture yourselves in a coffee shop as two old friends talking about life, how would you *explore* a difficult issue

between you? What different angles would you consider on
that particular issue?

4. Think of one knotty place in your communication where
you might have misinterpreted something he said or did. Voice
the possibility that you could have drawn a wrong or mis-
guided conclusion . . . maybe. Ask him, "What did you mean
by that statement [or that choice]?" Check it out, holding open
the possibility that, at least, his intent was different than how
it appeared to you.

How does this exercise affect (or not) the interpretation
being made? What further light comes into the picture?

5. The New Testament holds a few passages filled with relational wisdom. Paul's letter to the Colossians is one of those.
Read these verses a couple of times, asking God to highlight the
phrases most needed in your relationship with this man:

> But now you also, put them all aside: anger, wrath, mal-
> ice, slander, and abusive speech from your mouth. Do not
> lie to one another, since you laid aside the old self with
> its evil practices, and have put on the new self who is
> being renewed to a true knowledge according to the image
> of the One who created him. . . .

So, as those who have been chosen of God, holy and beloved, put on a heart of compassion, kindness, humility, gentleness and patience; bearing with one another, and forgiving each other, whoever has a complaint against anyone; just as the Lord forgave you, so also should you.

Beyond all these things put on love, which is the perfect bond of unity. Let the peace of Christ rule in your hearts, to which indeed you were called in one body; and be thankful. (Colossians 3:8–10, 12–15)

Write (or talk) about what stood out, why, and what it might mean to apply.

6. If you consciously shaped some piece of conversation that really matters to you in the form of *stroke*, *kick*, *stroke*, what would be the bare outline of that communication?

At some reasonable moment, try this tried-and-true way of stating something, which might come out with more sharp edges otherwise. What small steps of progress do you see?

Chapter 9

INTIMACY

1. With the man in your life, what are some of the moments that are "simply, and rather sweetly, good"?

2. Two people who are soul mates is a rare thing. Is this reality a comfort to you or a disappointment—and why?

3. The rigors of loving someone through times of hurt, misunderstanding, or disagreement mean that you choose to ride out the storms, rather than withdrawing from the relationship.

   Romans 5:3–5 speaks of particular benefits in the way God shapes your soul in this character-building process. Read what Paul is saying here:

   > We also exult in our tribulations, knowing that tribulation brings about perseverance; and perseverance, proven

character; and proven character, hope; and hope does not disappoint, because the love of God has been poured out within our hearts through the Holy Spirit who was given to us.

How can you see something redemptive in the process of learning to love in the dry seasons—as well as the easier times?

4. Name an example in the life of the man you love where you see that accepting his strength means accepting a corresponding weakness as well.

Reflect on Paul's words on this topic:

Now may the God who gives perseverance and encouragement grant you to be of the same mind with one another according to Christ Jesus, so that with one accord you may with one voice glorify the God and Father of our Lord Jesus Christ. Therefore, accept one another, just as Christ also accepted us to the glory of God. (Romans 15:5–7)

What does this look like in your relationship?

5. When your happiness is "under your own column on the emotional ledger," how do you approach life differently? How does that affect your relationship with this man?

6. The apostle John writes the most about what it means to love someone well:

> A new commandment I give to you, that you love one another, even as I have loved you, that you also love one another. By this all men will know that you are My disciples, if you have love for one another. (John 13:34–35)

Think of your relationship with this man. Try putting the words of Christ in your own words. What is Jesus saying about love, and what does "more of it" look like in this relationship?

7. At the end of your life, what would you want to be remembered for by the man you love? How would you want to remember him?

NOTES

CHAPTER 1: UNDERSTANDING YOUR INFLUENCE

1. Maybe you've heard the words sung by Randy Travis to "Forever and Ever Amen," about how love lasts forever, "as long as old men sit and talk about the weather, as long as old women sit and talk about old men." "Forever and Ever Amen," Paul L. Overstreet and Donald Alan Schlitz Jr. ©1987. Admin. by Don Schlitz Music/ Universal Music (ASCAP).

2. An insightful single friend of mine once observed that as much as women enjoy relationships with each other and as good as those can be, both the friendship and the conversation can "turn in on itself," as though something is missing. In her words, "no sperm comes." Again, the miniature reality of a larger picture.

3. "When a Man Loves a Woman," Andrew Wright and Calvin Houston Lewis ©1966. Admin. by Pronto Music/ Quinvy Music Publishing (BMI).

4. John and Stasi Eldredge, *Captivating* (Nashville: Thomas Nelson, 2005), 25–26.

5. Genesis 2:18.

6. "Family Research Abstract of the Week: Men Dying Alone," *Family Update, Online!* 7, no. 8 (21 Feb. 2006), World Congress of Families, www.worldcongress.org/WCFUpdate/Archive07/wcf_update_708.htm.

7. "Deperado," Glenn Frey and Don Henley ©1973. Admin. by Cass County Music/ Red Cloud Music (BMI).

8. This is a term that George Gilder coined in his insightful book on the psyche of men, *Men and Marriage* (Gretna, LA: Pelican, 1986).

9. These categories were developed through the generous insight and help of Ralph Ennis, the Navigators' intercultural expert. Ralph is coauthor of the Connect series, a breakthrough Bible study series

focused on life transformation for ages eighteen through thirty-five. For more information, see www.navpress.com.

10. Psalm 127:1.

11. For more information on what recent genetics studies on gender differences are revealing, see the work of genetics expert Huntington Willard of Duke University.

CHAPTER 2: WHAT MEN DO

1. It's not that women don't exhibit these characteristics, but we tend to identify with a different set of values, or you could say "a different aspect of tending the garden," such as *relationships, support, nurturing, community, mercy, harmony, beauty, communicating, stillness,* and *cooperation.* Our hormones and the way our brains are created have much to do with why we place a higher stake in these values.

CHAPTER 3: WHY MEN HURT

1. As Frank Pittman writes in his insightful book *Man Enough,* "[Men] escape to the sanctuary of male silence, away from the anxious world of emotions, from female-imposed sensitivity to the state of people's mind and the nature of people's relationships. [It is] a world to which men come just to be together, in the quiet, accepting company of men." (Frank Pittman, *Man Enough* [New York: Berkeley, 1993], 217–18).

2. Or as one man said, "Why do you think men play sports? It's our most established form of affirmation. You can pat another guy on the back and say, "Great shot!"

3. It has been said that the part of a woman's brain that assembles this information could be compared to an interstate highway, where a man's ability is analogous to a two-lane country road.

4. Louann Brizendine, *The Female Brain* (New York: Random House, 2006), 21.

5. Elizabeth Berg, *The Art of Mending* (New York: Random House, 2005), 170.

6. One of the best-selling and most enjoyable books about how men do life is titled, simply, *Man Enough* (Frank Pittman, *Man Enough* [New York: Berkeley, 1993]).

7. George Gilder, *Men and Marriage* (Gretna, LA: Pelican, 1986), 12.

8. Ibid., 10–11.

9. See David Murrow's book *Why Men Hate Going to Church* (Nashville: Thomas Nelson, 2004) for an insightful explanation of a man's longing for greatness, as well as the constant way he adds up achievements on his masculine ledger.

10. As you might suspect, I did not invent that metaphor. A man did. And the fear is eloquently accurate.

11. Pornography emasculates a man because it reinforces passivity. In three clicks of a computer, an air-brushed woman appears who makes him feel wanted and desired . . . and she won't ever ask him to take out the trash. Pornography lures a man in—and then strips his soul to shreds. It's the surest path to obdurate self-centeredness available. If a habit of pornography hangs in the background of your relationship with a man, then you will want to insist on taking radical steps to confront the problem for both of you.

12. John Eldredge, *Wild at Heart* (Nashville: Thomas Nelson, 2001), 93.

13. I have to admit that the one time I tried to put words to what a man feels about sex ([[need article title and date/page]], *Today's Christian Woman*), I had men calling me from Canada and Arizona asking how I discovered these insights, to which I could only explain, "I simply asked a few questions and listened." So it's there to be discovered.

14. Frank Pittman, *Man Enough*, 106.

15. Matthew 3:17.

16. Deuteronomy 7:7–8.

17. Richard Rohr, *From Wild Man to Wise Man* (Cincinnati: St. Anthony Press, 2005), 69.

18. Tim Keller, pastor of NYC's Redeemer Presbyterian Church, uses the wonderful phrase "living for the redemption of the other" in his marriage series. See www.redeemer.com for his sermons on marriage.

CHAPTER 4: HOW MEN CHANGE

1. 1 Samuel 19–31.

2. Genesis 32:22–32.

3. Paula Rinehart, *Sex and the Soul of a Woman* (Grand Rapids: Zondervan, 2005), 176.

4. Daniel Goleman, *Emotional Intelligence* (New York: Bantam Books, 1995), 50–51.

5. These findings are available through many sources, most notably

the work of Deborah Tannen, Daniel Goleman, and Louann Brizendine.

6. One litmus test for a good man is his sense of remorse when he actually does realize he's walked on your heart. A highly dysfunctional man will not care. He may perversely get an ego stroke by a woman's powerlessness. If that describes a man you are relating to, you might want to Google the word "narcissism," or even "narcissistic personality disorder."

7. As a woman, you don't want to make the mistake of confusing passivity with submission, thereby excusing yourself from a tough stand you need to take.

8. I recommend Walter Wangerin's book *As for Me and My House* (Nashville: Thomas Nelson, 2001) for an excellent discussion of seeing a relationship like a child you must carefully tend.

9. See Harriet Lerner's book *The Dance of Anger* (New York: Harper, 2005) for more help on how two parties make changes in the "dance" of their relationship.

10. This need is so male that Tom Wolfe could successfully title his book on pilots and astronauts with the immediately identifiable phrase *The Right Stuff.* (New York: Farrar, Strauss, and Giroux, 1979).

CHAPTER 5: EXPECTATIONS

1. Think of how World War II shaped the life and character of your father—or your grandfather. By age twenty, most men were wearing uniforms, given huge responsibilities, fighting a genuine enemy in a foreign land, staring sacrifice and hardship in the face, and coming home to a hero's welcome. There is a noticeable lack of shaping male influences now, and consequently, the process of growing up, of realizing who you are as a man, takes longer.

2. Genesis 2:19.

3. Genesis 2:23.

4. Genesis 3:7–9.

5. Ephesians 5:25.

6. The classic analogy, which serves well, is that no close relationship can survive well as merely a twosome because it's like a stool with only two legs. It's inherently unstable. When two Christians marry, they have the possibility and advantage of having an innately more stable relationship.

7. Matthew 7:13–14.

CHAPTER 6: RESPECT

1. Proverbs 13:12.

CHAPTER 7: CONFLICT

1. If anger takes a physical form or physical threat in any way, then it goes, almost without saying, that a couple needs a competent third party to help them build, step-by-step, a "walk-in closet"—a way to contain their conflict that addresses the actual issues in small increments.
2. Pittman, *Man Enough,* 246–48.
3. Brizendine, *The Female Brain,* 131.
4. For further insight, see Scott Stanley, Susan Blumberg, and Howard Markman, *Fighting for Your Marriage* (San Francisco: Jossey-Bass, 2001).
5. James 1:20.
6. Dr. Emersen Eggerichs, *Love and Respect* (Nashville: Thomas Nelson, 2004), 57.
7. Few relationships can sustain the combination of the absence of sexual intimacy and a lack of positive verbal communication.
8. Citing John Gottman's research on the communication of troubled couples, Daniel Goleman makes the point that women who live with criticism and contempt are far more prone to a range of health problems. Similarly, when a woman shows contempt or disgust four times in a fifteen-minute conversation, statistics show that the couple is likely to separate within the next four years. See *Emotional Intelligence* (New York: Bantam, 2006), 135.
9. 1 Peter 3:6.
10. Hebrews 13:5.

CHAPTER 8: GETTING THROUGH

1. When you make an appointment with each other to talk about a divisive issue, you are buying time to get the objectivity that would allow you more "freedom to explore."
2. Coffee shops are ideal for touchy conversations. It keeps things civil, and you can't be easily interrupted.
3. A general guideline is that it's best to avoid questions that begin with "why," as those come across as too pointed or accusing, in most interactions. Use "how" or what" questions instead. Also, aim for a

generous sprinkling of both verbs—feeling and thinking. So you ask questions about what the other person was feeling . . . and what he is thinking. Similarly, you want to include explanations of your own experience in terms of what you think and feel. Both of you will emerge with a more-rounded understanding.

4. Proverbs 17:27–28.
5. For further insight, see Stanley, Blumberg, and Markman, *Fighting For Your Marriage.*
6. 1 Peter 2:1.
7. Philippians 2:3–4.
8. John Gray makes the point that with men, it's better to ask, "would you" rather than "could you." That may sound like a niggling detail, but he's right. A man hears "could you" as a question of his ability . . . and "would you" as a vote of confidence. See his book, *Men Are from Mars, Women Are from Venus* (New York: Harper Collins, 1995).
9. Proverbs 12:18.
10. In the book *Strong Women, Soft Hearts*, I've written about the way that facing our own vulnerability turns upside-down our basic notions about strength and weakness as a woman. Strength is actually the amount of vulnerability you can offer in relationships (Paula Rinehart, *Strong Women, Soft Hearts* [Nashville: Thomas Nelson, 2005]).

CHAPTER 9: INTIMACY
1. Romans 15:5–7 ESV; emphasis added.
2. Charlotte Chandler, "Bette Davis Sighs," *Vanity Fair*, March 2006, 256–59.
3. Zephaniah 3:17 ESV.
4. I am not setting up "happiness" as the greatest goal in life. Rather, I am looking at the practical, everyday aspects of feeling good.
5. Deuteronomy 4:9.
6. Stanley and Patricia Gundry, eds., *The Wit and Wisdom of D. L. Moody* (Grand Rapids: Baker, 1974), 10.

AFTERWORD
1. Proverbs 2:2–3 NIV.

ABOUT THE AUTHOR

Paula Rinehart has touched women's lives through writing, speaking, and personal ministry for more than twenty years. A professional counselor and author of *Better Than My Dreams*; *Strong Women, Soft Hearts*; *Sex and the Soul of a Woman*, and the best seller *Choices*, Paula speaks at women's conferences and women's retreats focused on personal growth and intimacy with Christ. She lives with her husband, Stacy, in Raleigh, North Carolina, where Stacy directs an international ministry, MentorLink, which develops leaders in countries where the church is growing rapidly. Stacy and Paula served for more than twenty years with the Navigators. They are parents of two grown children.

For more information on conferences and retreats, contact Paula at paularinehart@mentorlink.org or contact SpeakUp Speaker Services at speakupinc@aol.com. Her Web site is www.paularinehart.com.

HAS THE DAY-TO-DAY BUSINESS OF LIVING ROBBED YOU OF PASSION AND VITALITY?

*P*aula Rinehart's *Strong Women, Soft Hearts* offers you hope and help. Paula writes as both a kindred spirit and a compassionate counselor to women feeling robbed of their passions and trapped by life's disappointing realities.

Using true stories, professional insights, and her own heartfelt wisdom—plus an assortment of practical exercises and questions in a newly expanded study guide—Paula helps you

* reconnect with long-lost dreams and refocus misplaced passion;
* develop a vision for the *big picture* of your life;
* discover when, how—and Whom—to trust.

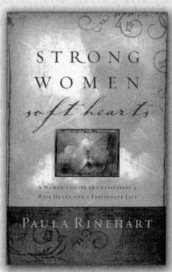

This book will help you listen and say *yes* to that call to become the strong, wise, loving, and fufilled woman you were always meant to be.

THOMAS NELSON
Since 1798

ISBN: 978-0-8499-0997-9

LET GOD TRANSFORM THE LIFE YOU THOUGHT
YOU WANTED . . . INTO SOMETHING EVEN BETTER.

*T*hough the story of your life may not be what you hoped for, there
are hidden treasures of grace waiting to be discovered. Face the fear
of being disappointed, find the freedom to love, and learn to rest in
the mercy of God with renewed confidence. *Better than My Dreams* shows
you that sometimes God offers a different sort of wonderful than the
one we have in mind.

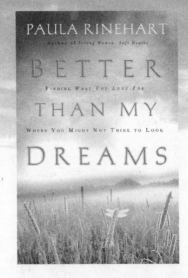

THOMAS NELSON
Since 1798

ISBN: 978-0-8499-1867-4